Marcantonio Spada is Principal Lecturer in Psychology at Roehampton University and a consultant cognitive behavioral therapist with the Community Alcohol and Drugs Service of the London Borough of Brent. He was previously principal lecturer in psychology and course director of the MSc in Cognitive Behavior Therapy at London Metropolitan University. An expert in cognitive behavioral therapy and therapy of problem drinking, he has worked as a clinician for several years in both private practice and mental health organizations. Marcantonio is a chartered psychologist, an accredited cognitive behavior therapist, and a registered psychotherapist.

The aim of the **Overcoming** series is to enable people with a range of common problems and disorders to take control of their own recovery program. Each title, with its specially tailored program, is devised by a practicing clinician using the latest techniques of cognitive behavioral therapy – techniques which have been shown to be highly effective in changing the way patients think about themselves and their problems.

The series was initiated in 1993 by Peter Cooper, Professor of Psychology at Reading University and Research Fellow at the University of Cambridge in the UK whose original volume on overcoming bulimia nervosa and binge-eating continues to help many people in the USA, the UK and Europe.

Titles in the series include:

OVERCOMING ANGER AND IRRITABILITY
OVERCOMING ANOREXIA NERVOSA
OVERCOMING ANXIETY
OVERCOMING BODY IMAGE PROBLEMS
OVERCOMING BULIMIA NERVOSA AND BINGE-EATING
OVERCOMING CHILDHOOD TRAUMA
OVERCOMING CHRONIC FATIGUE
OVERCOMING CHRONIC PAIN
OVERCOMING COMPULSIVE GAMBLING
OVERCOMING DEPERSONALIZATION AND FEELINGS OF UNREALITY
OVERCOMING DEPRESSION
OVERCOMING GRIEF
OVERCOMING INSOMNIA AND SLEEP PROBLEMS
OVERCOMING LOW SELF-ESTEEM
OVERCOMING MOOD SWINGS
OVERCOMING OBSESSIVE COMPULSIVE DISORDER
OVERCOMING PANIC
OVERCOMING PARANOID AND SUSPICIOUS THOUGHTS
OVERCOMING RELATIONSHIP PROBLEMS
OVERCOMING SEXUAL PROBLEMS
OVERCOMING SOCIAL ANXIETY AND SHYNESS
OVERCOMING TRAUMATIC STRESS
OVERCOMING WEIGHT PROBLEMS
OVERCOMING WORRY
OVERCOMING YOUR CHILD'S FEARS AND WORRIES
OVERCOMING YOUR CHILD'S SHYNESS AND SOCIAL ANXIETY
OVERCOMING YOUR SMOKING HABIT

All titles in the series are available by mail order.
Please see the order form at the back of this book.
www.overcoming.co.uk

OVERCOMING PROBLEM DRINKING

*A self-help guide using
Cognitive Behavioral Techniques*

MARCANTONIO SPADA

Robinson
LONDON

Constable & Robinson Ltd
3 The Lanchesters
162 Fulham Palace Road
London W6 9ER
www.constablerobinson.com

First published in the UK by Robinson,
an imprint of Constable & Robinson Ltd 2006

A copy of the British Library Cataloguing in
Publication Data for this title is available from the British Library.

ISBN 13: 978-1-84529-112-9

Important Note

This book is not intended as a substitute for medical advice or treatment.
Any person with a condition requiring medical attention should consult
a qualified medical practitioner or suitable therapist.

Printed and bound in Great Britain

10 9 8 7 6 5 4 3 2

Table of contents

Acknowledgments

I would like to thank all the clients who helped develop this book by trying out the exercises and strategies described. I am also grateful to Professor Adrian Wells, University of Manchester, whose inspiration and generosity have done much to shape and support my thinking. A special thanks goes to my wife, Ana, for her patience and loving support, and to my father and mother who have always been encouraging of my endeavours.

My thanks go also to the Lean Team Ltd for allowing me to reproduce material used in this book.

Preface

This book is a self-help guide aimed at dealing with problem drinking. It presents many of the well-established cognitive and behavioral therapy principles, skills and techniques that clients find helpful.

The book is divided into four parts: Part One looks at how problem drinking is defined and how it develops; Part Two explains how to go about building motivation to change; Part Three presents a step-by-step program for implementing change; and Part Four reviews a variety of strategies for maintaining change. I would recommend reading the entire book before starting the program as it will help you plan your time and efforts realistically. This is not a program that you have to carry out alone. Partners, family and friends can all help, particularly when implementing practical tasks. First, encourage them to read this book so that they can get a better understanding of the difficulties you face and the ways in which you are attempting to overcome them.

Working through this book from beginning to end, practising exercises and becoming confident in using the techniques described will take from four to six months. With some strategies that you find of particular benefit you are really looking at a life-long commitment. Try to have patience with yourself, as learning new sets of cognitive and behavioral techniques will take some time, and there will inevitably be setbacks along the way. With practice you should become increasingly confident that you can overcome your problem and you will be able to maintain your achievements by keeping your coping skills and good habits up to scratch and knowing how to deal with setbacks.

You will lose nothing by working through this book and I hope you find it helpful. It will be awe-inspiring if you manage to overcome your drinking problem and I wish you all the best for your future. If you make some progress but still feel there is room for improvement that is also good news. In both cases this indicates that the CBT (cognitive behavioral therapy) approach is of help to you. If you find that the book is not sufficient to fully meet your needs, consult a doctor or a CBT practitioner who can offer extra support. Needing to seek more help should not be taken as an indication of failure but simply as an acknowledgment of the complexity of your difficulties.

Introduction

Why a cognitive behavioral approach?

You may have picked up this book uncertain as to why a psychological approach, such as a cognitive behavioral one, might help you overcome your problems with drinking. A brief account of the history of this form of treatment might be helpful and encouraging. In the 1950s and 1960s a set of therapeutic techniques was developed, collectively termed 'behavior therapy'. These techniques shared two basic features. First, they aimed to remove symptoms (such as anxiety) by dealing with those symptoms themselves, rather than their deep-seated underlying historical causes (traditionally the focus of psychoanalysis, the approach developed by Sigmund Freud and his associates). Second, they were techniques loosely related to what laboratory psychologists were finding out about the mechanisms of learning, which could potentially be put to the test or had already been proven to be of practical value to sufferers. The area where these techniques proved to be of most value was in the treatment of anxiety disorders, especially specific phobias (such as extreme fear of animals or heights) and agoraphobia, all notoriously difficult to treat using conventional psychotherapies.

After an initial flush of enthusiasm, discontent with behavior therapy grew. There were a number of reasons for this, an important one of which was the fact that behavior therapy did not deal with the internal thoughts which were so obviously central to the distress that many patients were experiencing. In particular, behavior therapy proved inadequate when it came to the treatment of depression. In the late 1960s and early 1970s a treatment for depression was developed called 'cognitive therapy'. The pioneer in this enterprise was an American psychiatrist, Professor Aaron T. Beck. He developed a theory of depression which emphasized the importance of people's depressed styles of thinking and, on the basis of this theory, he specified a new form of therapy. It would not be an exaggeration to say that Beck's work has changed the nature of psychotherapy, not just for depression but for a range of psychological problems.

The techniques introduced by Beck have been merged with the techniques developed earlier by the behavior therapists to produce a therapeutic approach which has come to be known as 'cognitive behavioral therapy' (CBT). This therapy has been subjected to the strictest scientific testing and it has been found to be a highly successful treatment for a significant proportion of cases of depression. It has now become clear that specific patterns of disturbed thinking are associated with a wide range of psychological problems, not just depression, and that the treatments which deal with these are highly effective. So effective cognitive behavioral treatments have been developed for anxiety disorders, such as panic disorder, generalized anxiety disorder, specific phobias, social phobia, obsessive compulsive disorders and hypochondriasis (health anxiety), as well as for other conditions such as compulsive gambling, drug addiction and eating disorders like bulimia nervosa. Indeed, cognitive behavioral techniques have been found to have an application beyond the narrow categories of psychological disorders. They have been applied effectively, for example, to helping people with low self-esteem, those with weight problems and couples with marital difficulties, as well as those who wish to give up smoking or, as in this book, those with drinking problems.

The starting-point for CBT is the realization that the way we think, feel and behave are all intimately linked, and changing the way we think about ourselves, our experiences and the world around us changes the way we feel and what we are able to do. So, for example, by helping a depressed person identify and challenge their automatic depressive thoughts, a route out of the cycle of depressive thoughts and feelings can be found. Similarly, habitual behavioral responses are driven by a complex set of thoughts and feelings, and CBT, as you will discover from this book, by providing a means for the behavior to be brought under cognitive control, enables these negative responses to be undermined and a different kind of life to be possible.

Although effective CBT treatments have been developed for a wide range of disorders and problems, these treatments are not widely available and when people try to help themselves on their own they often do things which make matters worse. In recent years cognitive behavioral therapists have responded to this situation. What they have done is to take the principles and techniques of specific cognitive behavioral therapies for particular problems and present them in manuals which people can read and apply themselves. These manuals specify a systematic program of treatment which the individual works through to overcome their difficulties. In this way, cognitive behavioral therapeutic techniques of proven value are being made available on the widest possible basis.

Self-help manuals are never going to replace therapists. Many people will need individual treatment from a qualified therapist. It is also the case that, despite the widespread success of cognitive behavioral therapy, some people will not respond to it and will need one of the other treatments available. Nevertheless, although research on the use of these self-help manuals is at an early stage, the work done to date indicates that for a great many people such a manual will prove sufficient for them to overcome their problems without professional help. Many people suffer silently and secretly for years. Sometimes appropriate help is not forthcoming despite their efforts to find it. Sometimes they feel too ashamed or guilty to reveal their problems to anyone. For many of these people the cognitive behavioral self-help manual will provide a lifeline to recovery and a better future.

Professor Peter Cooper
The University of Reading

PART ONE

Understanding Problem Drinking

PART One

Understanding
Modern Processes

1

When does drinking become a problem?

People drink for a range of reasons and in varying amounts, primarily because they like the taste and the effects of alcohol and because drinking is a social activity – it is seen as harmless and entertaining. We use alcohol to toast a celebratory occasion or drown our sorrows, and throughout the UK almost every person has access to a local pub or bar. We are surrounded by images of people enjoying drinking – in newspapers and magazines, on television, on billboards and at the cinema. The Office for National Statistics estimates that some 90 per cent of the UK adult population consume alcoholic beverages on a regular basis, making consumption of alcoholic beverages second only to watching TV as the nation's favourite leisure activity.

For most adults it is a well established and acceptable part of their life. For a large minority, however, alcohol has the potential to ruin lives. In fact, at any given moment there are at least 3 to 4 million problem drinkers in Britain of whom around 35,000 will die every year due to alcohol-related problems. This is almost 20 times more than deaths caused by the misuse of all illegal drugs put together.

So when does drinking become a problem? Well, the answer is straightforward:

> *If your drinking causes you or someone else problems, in any area of your life, that drinking is problematic. Drinking may cause problems with health (both physical and mental), finance, work, the law, friends and relationships.*

This simple proposition implies that a drinking problem is not determined by fixed amounts of alcohol or set timings, but is rather a question of *negotiation*. Negotiation by the individual with himself or herself, family, friends, peers and society as a whole. The idea of negotiation can be illustrated by two classic examples.

Within the context of a relationship, one of the partners involved may be drinking a single shot of vodka a week, and the other may be a long-established teetotaller: this single shot may engender problems, and will need to be negotiated within the context of the relationship.

Twenty years ago, our ability to drive after consuming alcohol was assessed by our capacity to walk in a straight line. This has been renegotiated by society and it is now determined by blood alcohol level. If this exceeds a specified amount we are automatically deemed unfit to drive.

Telltale signs of problem drinking

The telltale signs of problem drinking fall into three straightforward categories: psychological, medical and social.

Psychological

Preoccupation with alcohol – a person with a drinking problem will think about alcohol to a greater or lesser extent during the course of the day. Questions such as 'When will I have my first drink?', 'When will I have the next?', 'Will the Millers drink?' will be common. These thoughts will usually cause distress and interfere with normal functioning, and might also prove difficult to resist or disregard.

Guilt – the reminders could be many: a dented bumper, a colleague's friendly advice, a partner's pleas and tantrums, the puffy eyes and blotchy skin.

Negative emotions – a drinking episode may be followed by a marked lowering in mood and/or an increase in anxiety. These same feelings may start to occur during hangovers and intermittently during the drinking period itself, especially if the drinking is heavy and continuous.

Medical

If problem drinking habits go on long enough, medical problems are very likely to emerge. These might take from a few weeks to several decades to develop. In exceptional circumstances some lucky drinkers may never be affected. It is possible for someone to consume a tremendous amount of alcohol, perhaps 3 bottles of whisky a week for 25 years or more, and yet to die a natural death, with brain, liver, pancreas and coronary arteries appearing normal. But the odds are strong that something will give. In fact, on average, drinking too much alcohol will reduce life expectancy by anything between 10 and 15 years. No part of our body escapes the effects of alcohol. Alcohol is a toxic drug and thus a poison to our bodies. Short-term effects of excessive drinking include upset stomach, diarrhoea, anaemia, dry skin and pins and needles; long-term effects include problems with attention, learning, thinking and memory, cancer (of the mouth, throat, breast, pancreas and liver), gastritis, ulcers, acid reflux, pancreatitis, hepatitis, cirrhosis, foetal alcohol syndrome in pregnant women and impotence in men.

Physical dependence on alcohol will show up as withdrawal symptoms when decreasing or stopping drinking. A number of signs may suggest that a person may be physically dependent on alcohol. These include daily drinking, drinking regularly and intermittently throughout the day, and drinking in the morning. Awakening with fears, trembling or nausea are also suggestive of dependence. Furthermore, cessation of or substantial decrease in drinking will result in the appearance of minor withdrawal symptoms such as tremulousness, nausea, vomiting, irritability and temperature. Such symptoms usually begin within 5–12 hours. More severe withdrawal symptoms, such as seizures, delirium or hallucinations, may also occur, usually within 24–72 hours of the cessation of drinking.

Social

Crime (violent crime in particular), absenteeism, accidents and unemployment are all telltale signs of problem drinking. In the UK, alcohol intoxication is involved in two-thirds of suicide attempts and more than 50 per cent of fire fatalities and homicides. It is also involved in 40 per cent of deaths through drowning, 40 per cent of serious head injuries and 30 per cent of domestic accidents. About one in six drivers involved in road accidents have blood alcohol levels above the statutory limit. Days lost from work because of alcohol-induced sickness are estimated to be in the region of a staggering 12 million per year. The social and financial cost of alcohol misuse is around £6 billion per year in the UK.

Is this book for you?

If you are concerned about your drinking or about someone else's drinking you can ask yourself the following questions:

- Do I often have more than a couple of drinks when I am alone?
- Do I need a drink at a certain time of the day?
- Has anyone ever criticized my drinking habits?
- Do I need a drink to make myself less shy in the company of others or to relieve other unwanted feelings?

If you have answered yes to any of these questions, you may want to look at your drinking habits. This book is likely to be useful to you. A note of caution: before continuing to read this book it is important to ask yourself whether you have *other* important difficulties in addition to problem drinking. Sometimes the presence of associated problems may hinder benefiting fully from a self-help program without some additional support. Ask yourself these questions:

- Am I feeling completely hopeless and down all the time?
- Has my drinking behavior contributed to legal action against me?
- Am I in severe financial difficulties and/or in danger of losing my job?

If you have answered yes to one or more of these questions, it may be prudent for you to look for professional support as well as following this book. It is particularly important that you do so if you often feel and/or have thoughts that life is not worth living. You may also find it difficult to overcome your drinking problem if you are feeling very down. Professional support and advice may also help you to minimize the impact of any legal and financial difficulties related to your drinking problem.

You can seek additional help through your doctor who can refer you to a Community Mental Health Team (CMHT) in the UK or to a specialist service. If you are referred for further help, portions of this book may still be helpful as an adjunct to both individual and group treatment.

2

How does problem drinking develop?

Terry's story

Terry, a 41-year-old man, was born in Manchester and moved to London in his late teens. He currently lives alone, is unemployed and is on long-term sickness benefit. In the past he worked as a carpenter, running a successful business employing more than twenty people. His problem started ten years ago when on holiday in Australia. He was involved in a traffic accident and was severely injured. He suffered from a fractured skull, broken ribs and a damaged spine and, as a consequence, he has chronic back pain and has been unable to work. Soon after the accident Terry started drinking heavily because he felt low and bored. He did not know what to do with his days as carpentry was the only trade he knew. Drinking was also a way to make the pain more bearable. Over time his energy levels began to drop and he found himself spending increasing amounts of time just sleeping, lying in bed, watching TV and in the pub.

Joanne's story

Joanne is a 28-year-old lawyer. Her parents, both doctors, had always emphasized the importance of academic and professional achievement. Joanne did very well at school, moved on to do well at university and became a lawyer. She is energetic and ambitious and often works a 55- or 60-hour week. She has little time for any activity outside of work during the week, so she tries to cram in all she can at the weekends. Recently, work pressures have been mounting (and work over the weekend has been increasing) and she has found that her alcohol consumption has escalated. She now finds it difficult to unwind and socialize without having a drink and has become accustomed to drinking by herself at home and occasionally binge-drinking at the weekend. She has tried a few times to cut down her drinking but has failed. She is starting to feel that the drinking is getting her down and affecting her mood and sleep.

There are no records of individuals born with an alcoholic beverage in their hand. Anyone who is experiencing a problem with drinking *must* have, at some stage in their life, learned to use alcohol in a risky and problematic manner. Problem drinking can thus be understood in terms of a simple, perhaps obvious, formula:

Problem drinking = Learned behavior

We first learn to use alcohol in a problematical fashion through social interaction. Learning to drink occurs as part of growing up in a particular culture in which the social

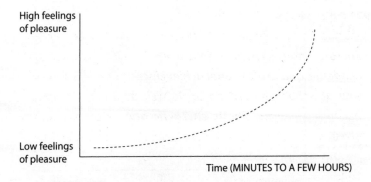

Figure 2.1 Alcohol's first short-term reward: increasing our feelings of pleasure (positive reinforcement)

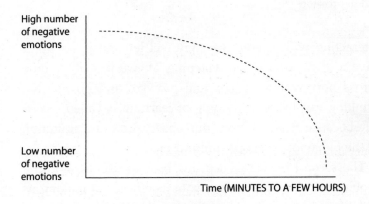

Figure 2.2 Alcohol's second short-term reward: numbing negative emotions (negative reinforcement)

influences of family members, friends, partners, peers and the media shape our behaviors and beliefs concerning alcohol. For example, we may see our parents reaching for a glass of wine to ease the stress of a hard day at work, or to enhance their ability to socialize at a party. When

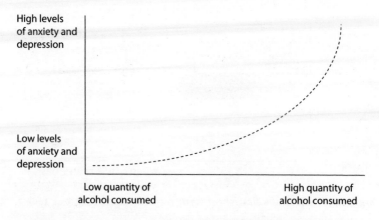

Figure 2.3 Alcohol's first long-term cost: increase in levels of anxiety and depression

interacting with friends we may feel left out if we don't have a drink, and when watching TV we probably come across portrayals of the sexual prowess and power that drinking can bring. This type of learning is called *modelling* because it arises from our observation and imitation of the behavior of people around us.

The second means of learning how to use alcohol in a problematical manner arises from its efficacy at making us feel relaxed: its reinforcement properties. As human beings we are wired up to engage in behaviors that gratify us. Drinking alcohol does just that. The reward we get from alcohol is actually twofold: it gives us feelings of pleasure, or a 'high', which is known as positive reinforcement (see Figure 2.1) and it numbs negative emotions, such as anxiety, anger, low mood and worry, which is known as negative reinforcement (see Figure 2.2).

The key point to note, however, is that the *rewards of*

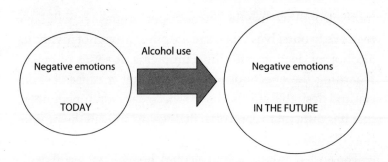

Figure 2.4 Alcohol's second long-term cost: increase in negative emotions

alcohol use are very *short term* (from a few minutes to a few hours, if that!). In addition, many people mistakenly believe that alcohol is a stimulant because it initially makes us feel less inhibited and more relaxed (it gives us a high), but in reality (especially in larger quantities) it is a powerful anxiety- and depression-inducing substance (see Figure 2.3)

On top of this, consuming alcohol does not offer any solution for dealing with negative emotions. After the drinking stops, the original negative emotions are still there but compounded by the anxiety and depression inducing powers of alcohol (see Figure 2.4).

Gradually, through this subtle process of giving in to short-term rewards at the expense of long-term costs, drinking alcohol may become the only well-learned habit for experiencing positive feelings and sensations and/or reducing tension and negative emotions. To make things worse, this habit may become *automatic* to such an extent that just smelling a pint of lager or seeing a pub will lead, before even noticing it, to a drinking spree. Over time the more alcohol we use the fewer opportunities we will have to prove to ourselves that there are other ways, not involving alcohol, of dealing with life's problems. A series of beliefs regarding the effects of alcohol (e.g. that it causes beneficial and desirable effects, that it is necessary for 'functioning', that it is difficult to control) will develop and aid the promotion of increasingly frequent and heavy use.

The added 'bonus' is that alcohol, being a powerful drug, will also engender physical dependence. Physical dependence will present itself in the need to consume increasingly large amounts of alcohol to get the same old rewards (the pleasure and the numbing effects) or even just to feel normal. One may no longer consume alcohol for pleasure, but feel tense, irritable, low in mood and in need of a drink to get through the day's natural ups and downs.

In conclusion, we learn to drink problematically by observing and interacting with others around us and by falling prey to alcohol's short-term capacity at making us feel relaxed and numbing our negative emotions. This is, unfortunately, at the cost of a long-term increase in those same negative emotions we dislike as well as in levels of physical and psychological dependence. A poor deal, to say the least! And a vicious cycle that is difficult to break (see Figure 2.5).

Cognitive behavioral theory looks in detail at the thoughts, behaviors and feelings that maintain problem drinking in an attempt to 'unlearn' this bad habit. Thoughts, behaviors and feelings are closely linked, often in the form of vicious cycles. The central aim of cognitive behavioral interventions is to interrupt these vicious cycles by identi-

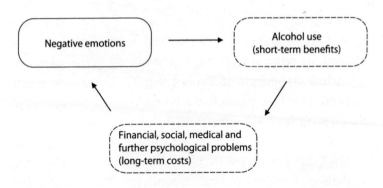

Figure 2.5 Simple model of the problem drinking vicious cycle

fying and finding ways to challenge and change unhelpful thoughts and behaviors.

One of the key strengths of cognitive behavioral theory is that it captures the person's unique experience of their problem and uses their language to understand personal thoughts, feelings and behaviors. Another key strength of this theory is that it has been widely investigated and is supported by substantial research.

PART TWO

Building Motivation to Change

3

Recognizing the problem and learning to monitor it

Assessing the severity of the problem

In the first part of this book we discussed drinking becoming a problem. The general point was that if your drinking causes you or someone else problems, in any area of life, then that drinking behavior is problematic.

What we did not highlight is the fact that there is also a *consumption* threshold for moderate drinking (which conversely implies there is one for problem drinking). This threshold is measured in units. One unit is equivalent to:

Half a pint of ordinary-strength beer or lager
One small glass of wine
A single measure of spirits

The Department of Health recommends that sensible drinking limits are no more than 3–4 units a day for a healthy adult man and 2–3 units a day for a healthy adult woman. This translates into a maximum of 21 units per week for men and 14 for women.

Surprisingly, many people, both with and without drinking problems, have only a very vague idea of how much they do drink. So the first thing to do is look in greater detail at your drinking habits.

Self-monitoring

I knew I had been using alcohol unwisely, but it was difficult to pin it down. Some weeks it felt as though I drank a lot, others it didn't. Then I started to keep track of what I was drinking and realized there was a pattern. A pattern I did not like the look of, a pattern that needed changing.   Joanne

An excellent way to get accurate information on your drinking pattern is to monitor it. This is important for three reasons:

1 It will give you a more tangible picture of the severity of the problem;
2 It will be the first step in beginning to learn how to manage the problem; and
3 Monitoring appears to help people reduce their drinking.

You can do this quite easily by keeping a record of when, where and with whom you drink, and how much you consume. Remember that this is *self-monitoring*: something you do *yourself, for yourself*. The key rule for effective self-monitoring is straightforward: every time that you have any alcoholic beverage anywhere note it down before you drink. Some people are quite comfortable noting down their drinks around others, some are not. But most people will not even notice you are doing it. Or, they will not think much about it. If you keep your records in a small notebook or a Palm Pilot it will make things even easier.

The Drinking Diary below is a typical tool used to record drinking patterns. It will help you to structure your record keeping. Use the blank diary to keep a note of your drinking for at least a *couple of weeks* before you progress to the next section of this chapter. When you look back over your entries you should find that you can answer the following questions:

1 When do I usually drink?
2 How much do I usually consume in a given drinking session and per week?
3 Where and with whom do I usually drink?

From your drinking diary you will be able to gauge if you are exceeding the recommended weekly amount. If you are, your problem will roughly fit into one of the following three categories:

AMOUNT CONSUMED PER WEEK	SEVERITY OF PROBLEM DRINKING
21–40 units	Moderate drinking problem
41–60 units	Substantial drinking problem
Above 60 units	Severe drinking problem

DRINKING DIARY: TERRY

Date:	Morning	Units	Afternoon	Units	Evening	Units	Total units
Monday			Pub with friends.	3	At home alone, watching TV.	5	8
Tuesday					Watching the snooker with Mark.	4	4
Wednesday							
Thursday			Pub with friends.	4	Alone at home sitting around doing little.	3	7
Friday			Pub with friends.	7			7
Saturday			Pub with friends.	5	Watching TV at home alone.	4	9
Sunday			Pub with Tony.	4			4

Total units this week: _____39_____

DRINKING DIARY

Date:	Morning	Units	Afternoon	Units	Evening	Units	Total units
Monday							
Tuesday							
Wednesday							
Thursday							
Friday							
Saturday							
Sunday							

Total units this week: _____

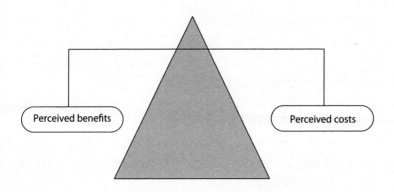

Figure 3.1 The drinking scale

It is also important to note that if you are drinking less than the weekly amount *but more than 3–4 units per day* you may still have a moderate to substantial drinking problem.

This book is primarily aimed at helping people who fall into the first two categories (moderate and substantial drinking problems). If you are experiencing problems in the third category (severe drinking problem), you may still find this book useful but you should consult a doctor and/or a CBT practitioner for further help.

Ambivalence

Finding out what your drinking behavior is actually like may give rise to a variety of emotions ranging from anger, low mood and deep upset to a sense of excitement and determination. On one hand, you may feel like throwing this book out of the window. On the other, you may feel a mounting readiness for a challenge and a newly found conviction in wanting to change your drinking behavior. In all probability you will be experiencing a mixture of all these emotions and *ambivalence* about whether you want to give up or reduce your drinking.

Ambivalence is feeling two ways about something ('I want to but I don't want to'). It emanates from competing desires because there are both benefits and costs associated with drinking (see Figure 3.1). If there were only costs nobody would be drinking!

What usually tends to happen to this scale is that as the weight begins to tip to one side you will tend to focus on the opposite side in an attempt to balance things out. You may experience ambivalence no matter which option is currently favoured. For example if you are abstaining, you might still feel ambivalent – there will be costs and benefits associated with it.

How these competing forces balance out at a given point in time will determine whether you indulge in or resist drinking. This is why ambivalence is confusing, frustrating and difficult to understand. Yet it is important to *persist*, despite this obstacle, and be tolerant and patient towards your own feelings of ambiguity. Remember that ambivalence is a normal and common component of many aspects of life, not just those associated with a drinking problem. It does not arise from a pathological personality 'lacking in motivation'. The challenge is to find ways of strengthening your willingness to change and gradually move away from ambivalence. Before we do this, however, we will briefly look at the process of change.

CHAPTER SUMMARY

- Regular self-monitoring is the first step in understanding whether you have a drinking problem.
- You may want to look at your drinking habits if you are exceeding the recommended amounts (14 units per week for a woman and 21 units per week for a man).
- If you drink more than 3–4 units on a single occasion you may also want to look at your drinking habits.
- Feeling ambivalent about your drinking patterns is a normal and common component of finding out that you may have a drinking problem.

4

Understanding change

Stages of change

The ambivalence about whether you want to give up or reduce your drinking and the readiness for personal change will largely depend on what stage of change you are at with your drinking problem. There are six key stages of change: pre-contemplation, contemplation, action, maintenance, slip and stability. These are illustrated in Figure 4.1.

The pre-contemplation stage

At this stage, you may not be aware that your drinking might be causing you problems. Alternatively, you may be thinking about the problematic side of your drinking but not be concerned about it.

The contemplation stage

In the contemplation stage you may acknowledge the link between drinking and the problems you are experiencing; you may also be trying to work out what is going wrong. At this point it is common to start pondering questions

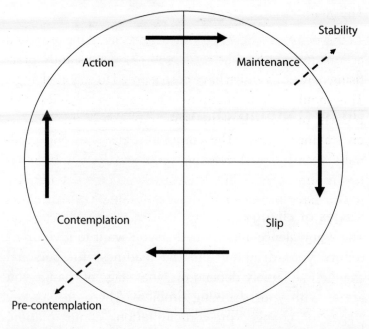

Figure 4.1 The process of change (adapted from Prochaska and DiClemente)

such as 'Do I have a problem with drinking?' or to consider altering your own behavior: 'I may have to do something about my drinking'.

The action stage

A serious commitment to action is usually formulated at this stage. You may decide to change your drinking patterns and take practical steps to do so. This may include getting specialized help or buying a self-help book!

The maintenance stage

At this point, you may be trying to implement the proposed actions for change. The focus will be on constantly prac-tising new skills which have been learned to enable change. This should help maintain new habits and behaviors that prevent problem drinking. The emphasis of this stage is on 'staying stopped'. The temptation of using alcohol grad-ually decreases and avoiding problem drinking becomes less central to your life. It is an important stage because if you have managed to drastically alter your drinking behavior for long enough you are likely to achieve long-term stability.

The stability stage

Getting to this point means that you have successfully learned new and more profitable behaviors, not involving problem drinking, and incorporated them into your repertoire.

The slip stage

For most, however, the next stage after maintenance is a slip. This is particularly common in the first three months of maintenance, where you may succumb to pressures to resume problem drinking. It is at this stage that the whole process of change starts again. You may find yourself back at a pre-contemplation, contemplation or action stage.

Why are the stages of change important?

What is important to bear in mind is that the process of change is cyclical. In other words, people go through the various stages *several times before succeeding* in dealing with problem drinking. The model implies that you can re-enter the cycle at any time following a relapse.

For example, if you slip you may go back to a pre-contemplative stage by avoiding issues you were facing before relapsing. Or you may return to the cycle at the contemplation stage, asking yourself questions such as 'Why did I slip then?' or 'What happened to my determination, focus and strategies?' There is also a possibility of re-entering the action stage: 'I know what happened and why. I am ready to have another go at tackling the problem now!' Or re-entering the maintenance stage: 'That was a slip and I have already stopped drinking. But I can see that the problems I had are likely to arise again when I have been abstinent for a long period.'

This is why motivation to change is not a static concept. Your motivation to change your drinking habits will alter as you move from one stage to another. For example, if you are at a pre-contemplative stage you are not likely to think that altering your drinking patterns is a worthwhile task, and hence both the ambivalence about drinking and motivation to change will be at a low level. In later stages you might find you are far more ambivalent, and the balance between changing and remaining where you are may be tilted towards change.

In the next chapter we look at ways of enhancing motivation to change with the aim of moving towards the *action stage*: wanting to change your drinking patterns and taking practical steps to do so.

CHAPTER SUMMARY

- Ambivalence about change will be dependent on the stage of change you are at with your drinking problem.
- There are six key stages of change (if you don't remember what they are go back and read the relevant section).
- What is important to bear in mind is that the process of change is cyclical.
- People go through the various stages several times before succeeding in dealing with problem drinking.
- Motivation to change is not a static concept: your motivation to change your drinking habits will alter as you move from one stage to another.

5

Enhancing motivation to change

Warning!
You may think you are motivated to change and ready
for action and can thus skip this section. My advice is
to read it and complete all the exercises. This will be
useful in cementing your motivation further!

A first step for encouraging change

Change is not easy if you have a drinking problem. Sometimes, even if you are extremely distressed about your drinking, it may seem much easier to remain where you are than to venture anywhere else. Ultimately, the responsibility for change will lie with you. If you are drinking you can continue to do so or you can decide to make a change.

The most direct way of enhancing motivation to change is to list the benefits and costs of continuing to drink, and the benefits and costs of changing your drinking. As a second exercise in this program, try to come up with your own list of benefits and costs, as Joanne has done in Table 5.1.

Table 5.1 A drinking decision balance sheet

CONTINUING TO DRINK		CHANGING MY DRINKING BEHAVIOR	
Benefits	Costs	Benefits	Costs
Helps me unwind	Damages my health	Feel better	What about my friends – will they find me boring
Gives me a high	Affects my job	Sleep better and feel more focused	How will I relax?
	Affects my mood	Have more energy	
	Affects my quality of sleep		

There are a variety of questions you can ask yourself to help you with this exercise:

- What are the good and not so good things about drinking?
- What could happen to me if I keep on drinking?
- What could happen to me if I stop drinking?
- What are the most important reasons for continuing to drink?
- What are the most important reasons for stopping to drink?
- Where would you like to be in two years' time?

A further step for encouraging change

This section contains an exercise for you to complete and information to help motivate you to change. The exercise (Exercise 1) involves doing two things: drawing up a detailed problem list and setting your targets. An example is given of a problem and target list completed by Terry.

EXERCISE 1

1 In the left-hand column of Exercise Sheet 1, under the heading 'Problems', draw up a detailed list of all the problems that you encounter due to your alcohol use. Ensure you include all the things about your drinking that are making you unhappy. Typical problems that occur are listed under 'Telltale signs of problem drinking' in Part One of this book.

2 Transforming problems into targets is a crucial and helpful first step in overcoming your drinking problem. Just thinking about your problems will not offer a solution or direction for getting better. Setting targets will give you something concrete to aim for and put you in a position where you might be able to find ways of achieving these targets. Turn to the right hand column of your exercise sheet and under the heading 'Targets' list one or more targets for each problem that you have identified. These will signal, once they are reached, that you are on your way to overcoming the problem. Make certain that your targets are as specific as possible. If they are too general, you will not recognize when you have actually reached them. Useful questions to bear in mind in helping you identify what your targets might be include:

- What would you like your drinking behavior to be like?
- What would you like to be doing instead of drinking?
- How would you like to think about your drinking?
- What would you like to be doing instead of spending so much time thinking about your drinking?

Try to be as realistic as possible about your targets, taking into account your lifestyle and any other circumstances that may make them difficult to achieve. A good question to ask yourself is:

- Would these goals be realistic if I were helping a friend overcome their drinking problem?

EXERCISE 1: TERRY
PROBLEMS AND TARGETS

Problems	Targets
Drinking has affected my friendships.	Abstinence.
Drinking has prevented me from finding a new job.	Abstinence.
Drinking has led me to get into unwanted fights.	Abstinence.
Drinking has caused serious debt problems.	Arrange a loan agreement with the bank, which covers living costs and debts, and which is to be repaid when I am earning a certain amount of money.
I end up spending more time doing unproductive activities after I've been drinking.	Allocate periods of time when I will research jobs on the internet or by reading the newspaper.
I end up spending more time in bed after I've been not drinking.	Increase the number of pleasurable activities each week, including individual exercise, reading, or listening to music alone. This should help me realize that a sober life is not boring!

EXERCISE 1
PROBLEMS AND TARGETS

Problems	Targets

Concerns about change

You will inevitably experience concerns about giving up or changing your drinking behavior – most, if not all people, do. Some of these concerns will have been highlighted in the drinking decisional balance sheet. What is important to bear in mind is that in nearly every case these concerns will turn out to be *unsubstantiated*. One of the most common concerns that problem drinkers have is that stopping drinking or changing drinking patterns will expose an empty life. This is because problem drinking behavior is likely to have occupied lots of their time and left little room for normal activities, or for thoughts and feelings unrelated to alcohol. So making these changes will almost certainly free up a considerable amount of both *thinking space* and *activity time*. When this happens, you will probably have little or no difficulty shifting your thoughts to other matters or finding other more pleasurable activities. Occasionally, however, it may not be quite so straightforward and life may appear to be extremely empty and lonely without alcohol. If this is likely to be a real problem, you will need a strategy to tackle it. (We discuss this strategy in Chapter 6.)

Resisting the *craving* to drink can also be a distressing experience. This may be another source of concern about change. What is important to note is that this is not usually as distressing as people predict it to be. Craving and associated distress can be overcome fairly quickly as you drink less often and get used to coping with problems and negative emotions in alternative ways. Some of the strategies presented later in the book will help minimize the distress linked to craving.

You may also be concerned that without drinking on your side you will be *unable to cope* with any problems that may arise in day-to-day life. This concern can make it very hard to give up your drinking behavior. It may also affect motivation to change. Hopefully you will discover, as you progress through this book, the many other more adaptive ways of dealing with life's problem and difficulties.

Persuading yourself to change

Unless you persuade yourself that change is going to be beneficial, you are unlikely to be fully committed to working through this book. You may be tempted to give up when things get difficult. This section suggests some exercises that will help you cement your commitment to change. Exercise 2 gets you to look at the advantages of changing together with any concerns you may have about change itself. It will also help you to weigh up the extent to which any of these concerns about change are realistic or unrealistic. Advice on dealing with realistic concerns will also be given.

EXERCISE 2

1 In the first column of Exercise 2 (left blank for you to fill in), under the heading 'Advantages', list all the advantages of changing that come to mind. Make sure you take into account all the problems that you identified in Exercise 1. Change will have an impact on many areas of your life. Think how it might positively affect your friendships, health, career, relationships and family. As well as pondering the immediate benefits, try to also think about medium- and long-term benefits of change.

2 Once you have covered the advantages, move on to the second column with the heading 'Concerns'. In this column, list all your concerns about change. Ensure once again that you consider all the problems that you highlighted in Exercise 1. Ask yourself whether change could have a negative effect on friendships, health, career, relationships and family. As well as immediate concerns, consider too whether there might be any medium- and long-term negative outcomes of change.

3 Once you have compiled the list, consider carefully what completing this exercise suggests. Like many others, you may find that the advantages of change greatly outweigh concerns you may have. Write your conclusions at the bottom of the exercise sheet under the heading 'Outcome'.

4 By now you should have identified at least one concern, if not several, about change. It is usually helpful to examine these in greater detail so that they do not get in the way of your commitment to change. Use the third column to respond to concerns. When doing this, think of the following questions:

- What would be another way of looking at this?
- Is there any evidence that this may happen?
- Do possible long-term advantages outweigh this risk, worry or problem?
- If this is likely to be a real problem, how will I deal with it?

Not all the questions will be relevant to each concern identified. Make sure you choose those that appear most appropriate.

5 Once you have responded to any concerns, go again through your initial conclusions written at the bottom of the exercise sheet under the heading 'Outcome'. Is there anything more to add? If there is, write it down. A completed exercise sheet provides examples of possible advantages, concerns and responses to those concerns that may be relevant to you.

EXERCISE 2: EXAMPLE
ADVANTAGES OF CHANGING, CONCERNS, AND RESPONSES TO CONCERNS

Advantages	Concerns	Responses to concerns
I will be able to stop using other drugs.	At some point, I will give in to a craving.	I have ridden out cravings in the past. There is no good reason why I cannot do it again. My motivation to stop drinking has increased, which will make it easier to resist cravings.
I will be able to get my studies completed.	I'll always have cravings for alcohol.	I used to have cravings for nicotine, cannabis or speed in the past and didn't have cravings for a while. It's likely to be the same for alcohol.
I will have a chance of a good career.	I'll always miss the highs.	The highs are obviously not worth it. It's unlikely that I 'll always miss the highs. I don't miss cannabis, nicotine or speed highs, although I did for a while when I first gave these drugs up. It's likely to be the same with alcohol. I may miss it for a year or so, and then I won't think about it much.
I will have fewer money problems.		
I will be able to be a decent boyfriend.	My life might become boring and empty.	Drinking has not resulted in an interesting and rich life. It has resulted in unwanted behavior, disruption and emotional pain and a limited solitary life. A life without alcohol is likely to be more interesting and fuller than a life with alcohol. I can organize and do interesting, pleasurable activities. I can get on with my work and probably get more out of it. I can have a relationship.
I will have the chance to feel good more consistently.		
My family will be pleased and worry less.	I don't like the idea of being a teetotaller.	I like the idea of being drug-free; alcohol is a drug just like cocaine or heroin. I don't think there's anything good about 'snorting like a man' or 'shooting up like a man'. Why should I think differently in the case of drinking excessively?

| I will be able to take responsibility for my life (e.g. finances, career, relationships, self-development, health). | People might dislike me or reject me – I may not fit in. | My friends won't reject me for not drinking, quite the opposite. The vast majority of the time I have mixed with work colleagues while sober and we've gotten on well; and my work colleagues are much, much more likely to take a dim view of me if I continue to drink than if I stop. People are probably less interested in whether I drink than I think they are. I can test out whether or not people will reject me by organizing social activities and recording the results. |
| | Work-related social occasions (e.g. conferences) may become difficult. | When I drink, I hardly ever participate in work-related social occasions. If I carry on drinking, I won't be going to any. But by not drinking, I can participate more and contribute more, especially at conferences, for instance. An end of term party or after conference 'drinks' may make me feel a little uncomfortable, although I have no evidence to think this. But I can always leave. I remember going to an end of term party one time and not drinking. I felt fine. |

Outcome

I can get through the cravings. They'll eventually more or less go away. Alcohol results in solitary bingeing and unwanted behavior. They'll eventually more my life interesting or full. If I am smart and put the effort in, I can have a largely pleasurable and productive life without alcohol. Most people don't care if I drink or not. Some friends want me to stop drinking. My work colleagues would prefer a productive and reliable colleague rather than an unproductive one.

EXERCISE 2
ADVANTAGES OF CHANGING, CONCERNS, AND RESPONSES TO CONCERNS

Advantages	Concerns	Responses to concerns

Outcome

The following exercise is designed to help you estimate how realistic any concerns you have about change may be. This will help you to get a better idea about what stopping drinking will mean or achieve in practice, and whether you will need to prepare a detailed plan to deal with any problems that may result.

EXERCISE 3

1 At the top of Exercise Sheet 3 write down a concern you have about changing and what you predict will happen if you overcome your drinking problem. Be as specific as possible and ensure that you write down what you think is the very worst thing that may occur.

2 In the section underneath rate how likely you think that the worst will actually happen, using a scale from 0 to 100 per cent (0 being 'not at all likely' and 100 being 'extremely likely').

3 In the left-hand column, under the heading 'Evidence for', list all the evidence you have that your concern is realistic.

4 In the right-hand column, under the heading 'Evidence against', record all the evidence which suggests that your concern may not be realistic. As before, you may find it useful to ask yourself the following questions when assessing the evidence for specific concerns:

- Have there been times when I thought this and it turned out not to be the case?
- What would my best friend say about this?
- Am I just focusing on the negatives because I am feeling down?

5 Ask yourself how realistic your concern appears now. To get a more concrete idea, rerate it on the 0 to 100 per cent scale. Ensure you write your rating at the bottom of the exercise sheet, under the heading 'Outcome'. You may want to write a summary of your conclusions.

If Exercise 3 suggests that *several* of your concerns about change are realistic, you will need to think carefully about change. It is not advisable to deal with too many *realistic* change concerns without additional help. You can seek additional help through your doctor. The doctor can refer you to a Community Mental Health Team (CMHT) in the UK or to a specialist service. If you are referred for further help, portions of this book may still be helpful as an adjunct to both individual and group treatment.

A word on drinking goals

At this stage you may already have a drinking goal in mind. It is either going to be abstinence or controlled drinking. Whatever drinking goal you choose is legitimate, but evidence shows that controlled drinking is more difficult than abstaining. Abstaining is straightforward – you just avoid drinking alcohol. Controlled drinking, however, is open to *deliberate* or *accidental* miscalculation of how much you may have drunk. In addition, because of alcohol's disinhibitory properties (its effect of reducing your inhibitions and disrupting the monitoring of behavior), you may not be able to keep to a prearranged limit even if you feel totally confident before you start drinking. Some people appear more successful at pursuing a controlled drinking goal than others. They usually (but not always) tend to be younger, be in employment, have a family around them, have only a short history of drinking problems and lower consumption levels before seeking help, and show no signs of physical dependence. Ideally you should:

EXERCISE 3: TERRY
EXAMINING SPECIFIC CHANGE CONCERNS

What do you predict will happen?
My life might become boring and empty.

How likely is it to happen? (0–100%)
50%

Evidence for	Evidence against
I often feel bored or low.	After I've been drinking, I feel extremely low for long periods of time.
Drinking is often a major part of many social activities.	My drinking and related activities are hardly a barrel of laughs.
	Anyone looking in would not say that drinking gives me an interesting and full life – quite the opposite.
	If I drink, I am unable to have a relationship.
	If I drink, I diminish my capacity to have a productive life.

Outcome

How likely do you think it is now that this will happen? (0–100%)
30%

Conclusions

I am more likely to have an interesting and full life without alcohol than with it. A problem at the moment is that I sometimes miss alcohol highs. But I have reason to think this will pass, given past experience.

EXERCISE 3: JOANNE
EXAMINING SPECIFIC CHANGE CONCERNS

What do you predict will happen?
I'll give in to a craving.

How likely is it to happen? (0–100%)
60%

Evidence for	Evidence against
I have given into cravings in the recent past and got drunk	I am working on my motivation to stop drinking. As a result my motivation is increasing.
	It took me several attempts to stop smoking. Ultimately, I resisted the cravings.
	I know that my drinking must change, and if I drink, I am simply making life difficult for myself in the long-run.

Outcome

How likely do you think it is now that this will happen? (0–100%)
30%

Conclusions

As my motivation to change increases, my ability to resist cravings will increase. There is no question that I must change my drinking, and abstinence for the foreseeable future is the safest option. I realize now that if I drink, I'm setting back my progress and making life difficult for myself. Realizing this helps me resist cravings. I have come through cravings for other substances in the past. There is no reason why I can't do it again.

EXERCISE 3
EXAMINING SPECIFIC CHANGE CONCERNS

What do you predict will happen?

How likely is it to happen? (0–100%)

Evidence for	Evidence against

Outcome

How likely do you think it is now that this will happen? (0–100%)

Conclusions

- Start off by trying to abstain for a period of three months

Once you have managed to understand the nature of your drinking problem and have built alternative resources to tackle what triggers it, you may *possibly* want to look at controlled drinking. The latter option is discussed in Chapter 15.

CHAPTER SUMMARY

- Identifying costs and benefits is the first step in the change process.
- The advantages of change will outweigh any possible negative outcomes or concerns.
- Some concerns may be unfounded, though some may not.
- It is usually better to put realistic concerns about change on hold until your drinking problem has improved.
- Evidence shows that controlled drinking is more difficult than abstaining.
- Abstaining may be a better initial goal when tackling your drinking problem.

PART THREE
Implementing Change

6

The cognitive behavioral model

In this part of the book we will start to make sense of, and challenge, the thoughts and behaviors that exacerbate and maintain your drinking problem. There is a wide variety of techniques that can be used to do this. These will be described in detail in the chapters that follow. By using these techniques and strategies you can often be successful at bringing your drinking problem under control. Don't forget, however, that your chances of success will very much depend on you regularly *practising* these techniques.

This self-help book is based on cognitive behavioral therapy principles. As mentioned earlier, the key idea of this therapy is that thoughts, behaviors and feelings are closely linked, often in the form of *vicious cycles*. The central aim of cognitive behavioral strategies is to interrupt these vicious cycles by identifying and finding ways to challenge and change unhelpful thoughts and behaviors. Before you can learn how to do this you will need to know how to recognize examples of your own vicious cycles.

The A-T-E-B-C analysis

The A-T-E-B-C analysis forms the starting point of the vicious cycles we will discuss later in the chapter. A-T-E-B-C describes the link between *activating events* (A), *thoughts* (T) and *emotions* (E) arising from these events, *behaviors* (B) arising from these thoughts and emotions, and *consequences* (C), both short and long term, of these behaviors. It can be difficult at times to identify As, Ts, Es, Bs and Cs and you may need to practice with several examples. Start by doing Exercise 4. An example of a completed A-T-E-B-C analysis follows. This should be of help when completing your own analysis.

EXERCISE 4

1 The first step is to identify a recent and specific event or circumstance (A) that resulted in you drinking. To help you identify this, ask yourself the following questions and record your answers under the heading 'Activating event':
   - When did it happen?
   - Where was I?
   - Who was I with?
   - What was I doing?
   - What was I thinking about?
2 Identify associated thoughts (Ts). Ask yourself the following questions and record your answer under the heading 'Thoughts':
   - What was running through my mind during the activating event?
   - What was I saying to myself?
   - What was I thinking about myself?

Thoughts or feelings?

It is sometimes difficult to distinguish between thoughts and feelings. In a nutshell, thoughts (e.g. 'I have no control' or 'I am a failure') can be directly challenged or changed in a variety of ways. Emotions (for example: anger, guilt, sadness) cannot. In cognitive behavioral therapy it is challenging the thoughts and associated behaviors that will indirectly change emotions and consequently help you tackle your drinking.

3 The third step is to identify emotions (Es). Ask yourself the following questions and record your answer under the heading 'Emotions':
   • What feelings did I have?
   • What did I do?
4 What behaviors (Bs) resulted from your thoughts and emotions? Write these down under the heading 'Behaviors'.

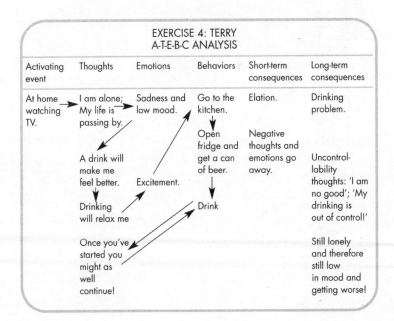

EXERCISE 4: TERRY
A-T-E-B-C ANALYSIS

Activating event	Thoughts	Emotions	Behaviors	Short-term consequences	Long-term consequences
At home watching TV.	I am alone; My life is passing by.	Sadness and low mood.	Go to the kitchen.	Elation.	Drinking problem.
	A drink will make me feel better.	Excitement.	Open fridge and get a can of beer.	Negative thoughts and emotions go away.	Uncontrollability thoughts: 'I am no good'; 'My drinking is out of control!'
	Drinking will relax me		Drink		
	Once you've started you might as well continue!				Still lonely and therefore still low in mood and getting worse!

EXERCISE 4
A-T-E-B-C ANALYSIS

Activating event	Thoughts	Emotions	Behaviors	Short-term consequences	Long-term consequences

5 What are the consequences of having chosen to behave in the way you did (i.e. problem drinking) – that is, what are the short-term benefits and the long-term costs? Write the benefits under the heading 'Short-term consequences' and the costs under the heading 'Long-term consequences'.

What you will probably have noted at this stage is that:

- Drinking usually results from thoughts and emotions and that these, in turn, result from activating events.
- Drinking is there because it provides short-term relief from these thoughts and emotions.
- However, drinking also exacerbates these thoughts and emotions in the long-term.

Now that you have carried out an A-T-E-B-C analysis, we can move on to see how it becomes a vicious cycle.

The vicious cycle

Figure 6.1 illustrates how a vicious cycle tends to work for drinking. This is adapted from the example A-T-E-B-C analysis in Exercise Sheet 4. Note how the Ts, Es and Bs alternate to create the vicious cycle.

In Exercise 5 you can turn your own A-T-E-B-C analysis into a vicious cycle format. Use the questions in Figure 6.2 and your own A-T-E-B-C analysis to help you.

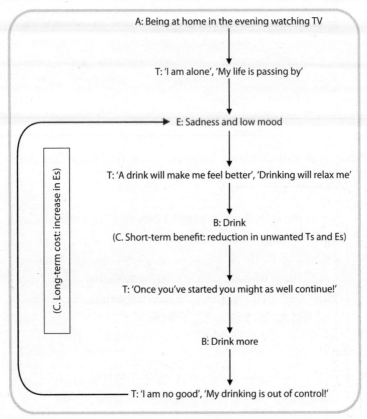

Figure 6.1 An example of a vicious cycle

EXERCISE 5

1 Fill in the A-T-E section at the top of Exercise Sheet 5.
2 Answer the other questions in Figure 6.2 following the arrows. Notice that your vicious cycle consists of a series of T-E-B-T-Es where certain thoughts are followed by certain emotions which, in turn, are followed by behaviors which may be followed by further thoughts and behaviors, and so on.

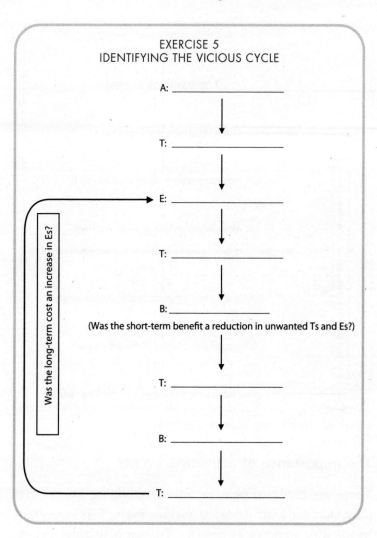

EXERCISE 5
IDENTIFYING THE VICIOUS CYCLE

A: _____

T: _____

E: _____

T: _____

B: _____
(Was the short-term benefit a reduction in unwanted Ts and Es?)

T: _____

B: _____

T: _____

Was the long-term cost an increase in Es?

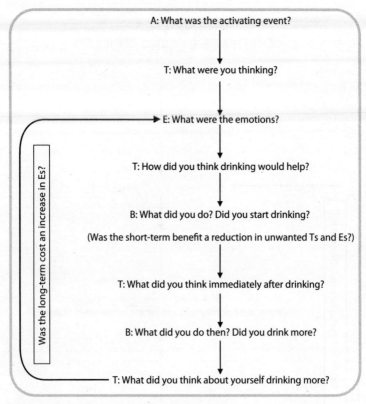

Figure 6.2 Identifying your vicious cycle

The importance of activating events

There are likely to be a *variety* of activating events that may start off your drinking vicious cycle. It is important to identify *as many as possible*. Typical activating events will include the sight and smell of alcohol, seeing a pub or bar, drinking friends, being at home alone and so on. In other words anything that has become *associated*, over time, with triggering drinking.

ACTIVATING EVENT DIARY						
Date:	Time	Drink	Amount	Activating event	Thoughts	Emotion
Thursday 5 August	18:30	Wine	2 glasses	At home before going out to meet new people at a restaurant	Will they like me?; A drink will make me relaxed	Anxiety
Thursday 5 August	20:00	Wine	6 glasses	Talking to people at the restaurant	I don't like these people. Why am I wasting my time and money with them?	Frustration Boredom
Saturday 7 August	18:00	Whisky	4 shots	Sitting at home	I am alone. Does anybody care?	Low mood

The only reliable way to find out which events kick-start your drinking cycle is to ensure that you keep a record of what goes on when you drink. The Drinking Diary that you completed at the beginning of this book will help you identify the amount of alcohol you are consuming and give you a rough idea of what you are doing and where you are when you drink. However, a more detailed recording system is needed in order to identify your personal *range* of activating events: the Activating Event Diary.

Note how, in this example, different activating events, thoughts and emotions led to drinking. If you keep records like these for a few weeks, you will begin to see *patterns* of activating events in your own life. The patterns here are fairly clear. The person drinks mainly in the evenings and towards the end of the week. Key activating events are meeting new people and being concerned about not being liked, not liking the company of particular people, and being alone at home during the weekend.

The following are classic activating events that you should look out for and simple strategies to start tackling them.

Places

It may be instantly obvious where your high-risk drinking places are, but it can also be subtle. Research has demonstrated, for example, that people are more likely to drink heavily in places where:

- certain kinds of music are played
- competition is high for sexual partners
- other people are drinking heavily
- the lights are turned down.

If you discover a place that activates your drinking you may wish to avoid it for some time. It does not mean you will never go there again, but before you do, you may want to rehearse your CBT skills. People who successfully moderate their drinking often avoid high-risk situations for a while. If for some reason you are not able or not willing to do so you will have to figure out how to manage your drinking while you are there. The following are things you can do to break old habits when drinking.

- If you are going out take somebody with you who is unlikely to drink or will make it harder for you to drink.
- Take a limited amount of money with you.
- Go out at different times of the day and/or week.
- At home, move things around to change your environment (different lighting, rearrange furniture).
- Change what you drink or the people you drink with.
- Keep only limited amounts of alcohol in the house.

Other people

Certain people can make it more likely that you will drink excessively. People who drink heavily, ridicule drinking in moderation, push drinks or buy rounds; people who make you feel anxious (and drinking provides a way to relax). Sometimes drinking happens simply because of what you do with a particular person. If, for example, you are with someone who likes to go from pub to pub it will be harder to avoid drinking.

Conversely, there will be other people with whom you are more likely to drink moderately or not at all. These will include moderate drinkers, abstainers or simply people

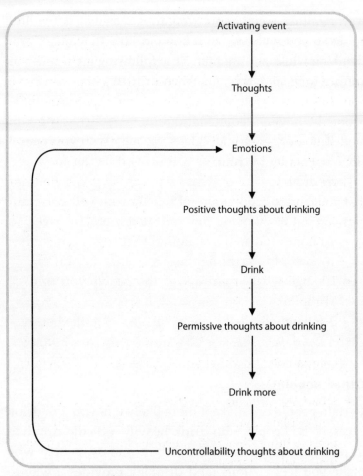

Figure 6.3 The problem drinking model

you do not feel anxious with. And there may be times when you restrain your alcohol consumption to make a favourable impression on someone (e.g. your boss, the doctor).

There is a good chance you are already thinking about which people in your life may influence your drinking. As with all other exercises in this book, a useful way to find out how people affect your drinking is to record it. You should try to keep track of who you are with when you are drinking and how much you drink. After you have done this for a fortnight or so examine the results. Are there people with whom you tend to drink excessively, drink in moderation or not drink with at all? What about if you are alone or in a large group?

There are a variety of things you can do if you find out that you tend to drink excessively in the company of certain individuals:

- *Try to cut down your drinking and see what happens.* The other person may also start reducing their drinking.
- *Ask for help.* This will require you to let your companion know that you are trying to reduce your alcohol intake.
- *Spend less time together.* If you do this ensure that you explain that it is not to do with disliking the person but rather with needing to be away from places where temptation is strong.

Time

A big factor that can affect drinking patterns is time. Most people who drink excessively will do so on certain days of the week and at certain times of the day. Evenings, weekends, holidays and special occasions, such as parties and weddings, are likely to involve heavier drinking. By now you should know when you drink by looking through your diaries. The key tip is to impose a firm time limit on your drinking. This may range from not drinking to moderate drinking. If you decide to aim for moderate drinking, set a clear boundary: don't drink before 7pm during the week or 9pm at the weekend, and don't speed up your drinking to compensate for the reduced amount of time. Write your targets on a card and ensure that you carry it with you at all times. You may also want to print it out and stick it on a wall or cupboard door. More techniques on controlled (i.e. moderate) drinking are discussed in Chapter 15.

Summary

You should by now have a clearer idea of the 'mechanical' nature of drinking problems. In fact, any of your vicious cycles can be *roughly* transposed into a template or model of problem drinking. This is shown in Figure 6.3. In this model an activating event triggers different types of thoughts (and associated emotions). These in turn elicit *positive thoughts* about drinking (e.g. 'A drink will make me feel better') which help kick-start drinking episodes. Once alcohol use is initiated it is kept going by *permissive thoughts* about drinking (e.g. 'Once you've started you might as well continue!'). Eventually (be it during a hangover or a drinking episode itself) *uncontrollability thoughts* about drinking (e.g. 'My drinking is out of control') come to the fore ('uncontrollability thoughts' are thoughts that you cannot control your drinking). These are key in maintaining the vicious cycle because they generate additional negative emotions (e.g. self-blame) thus increasing the chances of triggering a new drinking episode.

In the chapters that follow we will focus on identifying and challenging all these sets of thoughts and related behaviors. Don't be disheartened if you found the exercises in this chapter difficult. Go over them again, with the related examples, until you feel comfortable with them. You may need to practice them several times before you are confident of identifying activating events, thoughts, emotions and behaviors, and understand how they are interlinked.

CHAPTER SUMMARY

- As are activating events, Ts are thoughts, Es are emotions, Bs are behaviors and Cs are consequences (short and long term).
- The A-T-E-B-C analysis forms the basis of the vicious cycles that maintain problem drinking behavior.
- It is important to distinguish between thoughts, which can be directly challenged, and feelings, which cannot.
- Note that the vicious cycle consists of a series of T-E-B-T-Es, where certain thoughts are followed by certain emotions and behaviors, which may be followed by further thoughts, emotions and behaviors, and so on.
- Any vicious cycles can be roughly transposed into a template or model of problem drinking (see Figure 6.3).
- There are a variety of activating events, thoughts and behaviors that fuel problem drinking behavior. These can be challenged in order to overcome problem drinking.

7

Challenging uncontrollability thoughts about drinking

Uncontrollability thoughts about drinking are key in *maintaining* the problem drinking vicious cycle. In this chapter you will learn to identify and challenge these thoughts. Take a look at some of the most typical ones below:

- I have no control over my drinking.
- I cannot stop myself.
- My drinking persists no matter what I do.
- Drinking controls my life.

If you believe that you cannot control your drinking, you will probably have good reasons for thinking this! Exercise 6 will help you identify what it is that makes you think you cannot control your drinking. An example of a completed exercise follows.

EXERCISE 6

1 At the top of Exercise Sheet 6 write down typical uncontrollability thoughts you experience. These thoughts are likely to occur during and after your drinking episodes. Try to use your own words as far as possible.

EXERCISE 6: JOANNE
EVIDENCE FOR AND AGAINST UNCONTROLLABILITY THOUGHTS ABOUT DRINKING

Uncontrollability thoughts	Belief in each thought (0–100%)
(a) I always drink, even if I'm really tired and have to work the next day.	90%
(b) Once I've started drinking, there'll always be a good chance I'll either lose control over my intake of alcohol or switch to other drugs.	100%
(c) I always drink after work, even if I'm alone or it's really late.	90%

Evidence for	Evidence against
(a) (i) I drink to 'unwind' after a long day; (ii) I drink to remind myself I'm not at the office; (iii) I drink to satisfy desires to get high.	(a)(i) Before I started this job, I didn't drink to 'unwind'. During periods of abstinence, I've felt stressed. Sometimes, while not abstinent, I've felt very stressed but not started drinking in response.
(b) Many times, when I hadn't planned to, I've not been able to stop drinking and/or switched to other drugs (e.g. I prepared a presentation. The night before the presentation I went for a drink with a friend. He went home after 2 or 3 pints. I compulsively continued to drink and failed to give the presentation I'd prepared over the weekend).	(a)(ii) I have plenty of other interests that I could spend time on to remind myself that I'm not at work (e.g. go to cinema, read, listen to music, go running, or watch TV).
(c) I have often started drinking at midnight and avoided going straight to bed just so that I can 'relax'.	(a)(iii) Sometimes, while abstinent, I've wanted to get drunk but not started drinking. Sometimes, while not abstinent, I've wanted to get high but not started drinking.

(b) I sometimes drink moderately. For instance, I've sometimes been with friends in a pub and successfully limited my intake to a couple of drinks.

(c) Before this job, I didn't drink to 'relax'. Since I started it, I've sometimes needed to relax but haven't started drinking. After several late nights of drinking, I stop but feel more tired and stressed out.

Outcome

With a commitment to abstinence, I have a large amount of control over the first drink. When not abstinent, I can probably reduce the problem of my drinking at the drop of a hat by putting myself under less pressure, developing better life skills, and doing more fun, rewarding activities. The fact that I sometimes drink moderately shows that I have some control over my intake of alcohol once I've started to drink. I may well be able to expand this control.

Rerating of belief in each thought (0–100%)

(a) I always drink, even if I'm really tired and have to work the next day. (60%)

(b) Once I've started drinking, there'll always be a good chance I'll either lose control over my intake of alcohol or switch to other drugs. (80%)

(c) I always drink after work, even if I'm alone or it's really late. (70%)

EXERCISE 6
EVIDENCE FOR AND AGAINST UNCONTROLLABILITY THOUGHTS ABOUT DRINKING

Uncontrollability thoughts	Belief in each thought (0–100%)

Evidence for	Evidence against

Outcome

Rerating of belief in each thought (0–100%)

2 Rate your belief in each thought on a scale of 0–100 per cent, with 0 being no belief in the thought and 100 being completely convinced by the thought.

3 What evidence is there for and against your thoughts of uncontrollability? Typical evidence of lack of control (for) may include:

- drinking all the time
- hangovers
- not being able to stop once you start drinking
- drinking at any given opportunity.

Ensure that you make a list of all this evidence under the heading 'Evidence for'. The next step is to examine this evidence more carefully. You may be misinterpreting the evidence relevant to your drinking. The questions you have to ask yourself to challenge the evidence for lack of control (against) over drinking are the following.

- Is the evidence for lack of control over my drinking true 100 per cent of the time?
- Is there evidence that it might not be true 100 per cent of the time?
- Do I really drink every time there is an opportunity?
- Have there been times when I have not experienced a hangover?
- Can I recall one episode when I stopped drinking once I had started?
- Have there been times when I could have drunk and I did not do so?

Write your evidence in the right hand column of the worksheet under the heading 'Evidence against'. Make sure you challenge and re-interpret one piece of evidence at a time.

4 At this stage begin to consider what the evidence suggests. Write a brief summary of your conclusions under the heading 'Outcome'. After you have done this rerate how much you believe in your initial thoughts.

By now you will probably have realized that there is not much evidence to support some of your uncontrollability thoughts. Despite this, you may still have doubts that you can have some control over your drinking. This is because you are likely to have some reservations about the *new thought* that you *can* control your drinking. These reservations are natural and are usually expressed in the form of 'yes . . . but' sentences. A typical example would be: '*Yes*, I know I can control my drinking, *but* only when I am at work.' Giving up uncontrollability thoughts is not easy. After all, there is a good reason why they are there. The reason is that they take away responsibility from you. A very important part of successfully tackling your drinking problem will be that of accepting that you are responsible for what you do and that you can do things differently if you so wish. Hopefully, the final exercises in this chapter will help you strengthen the belief that you do have some control over your drinking.

One way to increase your confidence in the new thought 'I can control my drinking' is to go out and test it. You must become a scientist and carry out a *behavioral experiment* to prove or disprove this thought. The aim of the experiment is to build up your own confidence in the new thought.

Every drinking problem is different. So you will need to design and carry out the experiment that will work for you and ensure that the experiment is graded (i.e. you should start from a situation where it will be relatively straightforward to confirm that you do have control, and gradually build up to the more difficult situations). Over time, you should be able to tackle the most difficult situations.

Exercises 7 and 8 contain the drinking postponement experiment.

EXERCISE 7

1 Begin by identifying all the situations in which you find it difficult not to drink and list them on Exercise Sheet 7 under the heading 'Situation'.

2 Under the heading 'Difficulty' rate each situation on a scale of 0–100 per cent, with 0 being 'not at all difficult' and 100 being 'extremely difficult'. Rank the situations in ascending order of difficulty under the heading 'Rank'. A sample hierarchy of difficult situations follows. Make sure that the rankings you have given reflect the difficulty of the situations and you are ready to carry out the experiment in Exercise 8.

EXERCISE 8

1 Write, in your own words, the thought (e.g. that you cannot control your drinking) you are going to test at the top of Exercise Sheet 8 and then rate your belief that the thought is true on a scale of 0–100, with 0 being 'I do not believe this thought' and 100 being 'This thought is true.' Make sure you choose the rating that reflects your belief in the thought before continuing the experiment.

2 Start from the easiest situation and write what you plan to do in the left hand column under the heading 'Experiment to test thought'. In order to increase the probability of success, ensure

EXERCISE 7: EXAMPLE
HIERARCHY OF DIFFICULT SITUATIONS

Situation	Difficulty (0–100%)	Rank
Being home alone.	100%	4
Walking past the pub on the way home.	80%	1
Walking past the corner shop on the way home.	90%	2
Feeling upset or bored.	95%	3

EXERCISE 7
HIERARCHY OF DIFFICULT SITUATIONS

Situation	Difficulty (0–100%)	Rank

EXERCISE 8: EXAMPLE
DRINKING POSTPONEMENT EXPERIMENT

Thought to be tested

'My drinking is uncontrollable.'

			Belief in the thought (0–100%)		
			95%		
Experiment to test thought	Possible problems	Strategies to deal with problems	Date of experiment	Experiment outcome	Belief in the thought (0–100%)
To walk past the pub on the way home and not go inside for ten days.	I might meet a friend who will ask me to go for a drink.	Say no.	The week commencing	The strategies were of great help.	My drinking is uncontrollable. – 20%.
	I will crave a drink.	3 March. I will wait and see if the craving goes away.		I only once met guy I often drink with and told him I was not up for it.	
	There might be a football game on that I will want to see.	Change route on that day ensuring that you do not pass the pub.		I had a strong craving on a few occasions but waited for it to go away and went for a long walk.	
				The thought that my drinking is uncontrollable is not always true – I seem to have a choice and ways of doing things that actually help me to control it!	

EXERCISE 8
DRINKING POSTPONEMENT EXPERIMENT

Thought to be tested			Belief in the thought (0–100%)		
Experiment to test thought	Possible problems	Strategies to deal with problems	Date of experiment	Experiment outcome	Belief in the thought (0–100%)

that you think about possible problems. Write these under the heading 'Possible problems'. Then write down how you plan to deal with these problems (if they do occur!) under the heading 'Strategies to deal with problems'.

3 Carry out the drinking postponement experiment, ensuring that you start from the easiest situation. Record both the date and details of the outcome under the heading 'Experiment outcome' and rerate the belief in the thought that you cannot control your drinking on the usual 0–100 per cent scale. You are now ready to repeat the procedure for the next most difficult situation. Continue until you reach the top of your hierarchy. This whole process may take a few weeks, and don't forget that only repeated practice will help you to attain long-term changes in your drinking behavior.

What happens if things do not work out?

There is no need to panic if the postponement experiment goes wrong. This is likely to happen, especially at the beginning, when you are still practising how to carry it out. A negative outcome can be as useful as a positive one. It does not imply that you have no self-control but simply tells you that you need to take a closer look at your plan and ensure that you carry out a revised experiment utilizing what you have learned. In order to do this you will need to pinpoint what the problem was. The key questions to ask yourself are:

- Was the task too difficult?
- Are my expectations too high?
- What thoughts did I have?
- What did I learn from this?
- What can I do differently?

CHAPTER SUMMARY

- Uncontrollable thoughts are very important in problem drinking.
- The common type of evidence for uncontrollability involves thinking that you drink all the time and on every occasion.
- You probably have evidence that you cannot control your drinking as well as evidence that you can.
- You need to become conscious of the fact that you do have some degree of control over your drinking and that you are responsible for choosing whether to drink or not.
- The postponement of drinking experiment can be employed to confirm and strengthen your sense of control. A negative outcome is just as useful as a positive one and a necessary step for change.

8

Challenging permissive thoughts about drinking

Once you have identified and challenged thoughts that you cannot control your drinking, it is important to tackle those thoughts that keep drinking going once it is started: permissive thoughts. Examples of these types of thought include:

- I will just have one more drink.
- I have to drink at this moment.
- Another drink won't harm me.
- Now that I have started drinking, I might as well carry on.
- This is the last time I will be drinking so I should have all I want.
- I will start afresh tomorrow.

It is crucial to learn to identify these permissive thoughts 'on-line' (i.e. as they are occurring). However, recognizing them is not straightforward and you will need to practice exactly as you have done with uncontrollability thoughts about drinking. Exercise 9 will help you keep a record of the permissive thoughts in situations where you drink. An example of a completed exercise follows.

EXERCISE 9

1 Write down the activating event of your drinking episode on Exercise Sheet 9. Run through the questions at the bottom of the table under the heading 'Activating event'.

2 Under the heading 'Feelings and sensations' write down the feelings (e.g. anxiety, sadness, worry) and sensations you noticed before the drinking escalated.

3 Under the heading 'Permissive thoughts' write down all the thoughts you had before the drinking got out of control. Make sure you identify, and highlight, the key thought (the thought that is most likely to increase the probability that you continue drinking).

Practice doing Exercise 9 whenever possible over the next month. Don't forget that practice will make it easier to identify these thoughts.

Both identifying thoughts and challenging them takes practice. There are eight key familiar questions you can ask yourself that will be useful in challenging permissive thoughts:

1 Do these thoughts make it easier or harder to drink?
2 What would I say to someone else?
3 What have I learned from drinking in the past that could help me now?

EXERCISE 9: TERRY
RECOGNIZING PERMISSIVE THOUGHTS ABOUT DRINKING

Activating event	Feelings and sensations	Permissive thoughts
On a Saturday, I was walking alone along Regent's Park canal. I'd passed several pubs and booze shops. I had a strong desire to drink, stopped and had one.	Bored, frustrated and worried.	I've only got £40. So I can't do too much damage.
	Slightly elated from the alcohol, guilt.	I can start afresh tomorrow.
During my slip period, on one occasion, I went into a pub with the intention of drinking no more than two pints of beer. I drank two pints.	Bored, frustrated and worried.	I've got to drink more.
	Slightly elated from the alcohol, guilt.	Another few drinks won't do any harm.

EXERCISE 9
RECOGNIZING PERMISSIVE THOUGHTS ABOUT DRINKING

Activating event	Feelings and sensations	Permissive thoughts
When did it happen? Where were you? What were you doing? What were you thinking about?	What feelings and body sensations did you notice?	What were you saying to yourself that made it easier to keep drinking? Highlight the key thought that makes it most likely you will continue drinking.

4 Am I being misled by my feelings?
5 What are the consequences of thinking in this way?
6 What could I say to myself that would make it easier to stop drinking?
7 What would someone else say about this thought?
8 Is this situation similar to past situations?

Exercise 10 extends this exercise to include additional information for challenging the permissive thoughts you have been noting down. An example of a completed exercise follows.

EXERCISE 10

1 Write down the activating event of your drinking episode, the associated feelings and sensations, and the permissive thoughts on Exercise Sheet 10. Identify the key permissive thought and highlight it.
2 Under the heading 'Evidence not supporting the thought' write down all the evidence that suggests that the thought is not true. Use the eight questions listed above for challenging the permissive thoughts.
3 Under the heading 'Alternative thought' record an alternative and more balanced thought. Again, use the eight questions for challenging the permissive thoughts.
4 Rate how much you believe the alternative thought to be true on a scale of 0–100 per cent, with 0 being no belief in the thought and 100 being completely persuaded by the thought.

It is important to challenge your thoughts as often as you can whether they are uncontrollability, permissive or positive

EXERCISE 10: TERRY
RECOGNIZING AND CHALLENGING PERMISSIVE THOUGHTS ABOUT DRINKING

Activating event	Feelings and sensations	Permissive thoughts	Evidence not supporting the thought	Alternative thought	Belief in alternative thought
On a Saturday, I was walking alone along Regent's Park canal. I'd passed several pubs and booze shops. I had a strong desire to drink, stopped and had one.	Bored, frustrated and worried.	I've only got £40, so I can't do too much damage.	I have borrowed money from friends before.	I can borrow money; even if I only spent £40, I'd be strengthening a disposition to drink when feeling bad or bored.	95%
During my slip period, on one occasion, I went into a pub with the intention of drinking no more than two pints. I drank two pints.	Slightly elated from the alcohol, guilt.	I can start afresh tomorrow.	During my 10 week slip period, I had this thought many times, and yet I found it extremely difficult to stop drinking and stay stopped.	Past experience tells me that I'm unlikely to be able to 'start afresh tomorrow'. It isn't that easy. First, the morning after, I'll feel terrible and want to blot that out. Second, I'll be reinforcing a disposition to drink.	97%
	Bored, frustrated and worried.	I've got to drink more.	On occasions, in the past, I have stopped drinking after a few pints.	Past experience suggests that I can stop drinking after two pints. I'll feel less guilt if I stop drinking now than if I carry on and no doubt behave badly.	93%
	Slightly elated from the alcohol, guilt.	Another few drinks won't do any harm.	On many occasions in the past, 'another few drinks' has led to out of control drinking together with regrettable bad behavior.		99%

EXERCISE 10
RECOGNIZING AND CHALLENGING PERMISSIVE THOUGHTS ABOUT DRINKING

Activating event	Feelings and sensations	Permissive thoughts	Evidence not supporting the thought	Alternative thought	Belief in alternative thought
When did it happen? Where were you? What were you doing? What were you thinking about?	What feelings and body sensations did you notice?	What were you saying to yourself that made it easier to keep drinking? Highlight the key thought that makes it most likely you will continue drinking.	Use the eight questions above to challenge your thought.	Note the alternative more helpful thought.	Rate how much you believe this thought to be true on a scale from 0–100%.

thoughts (which we look at next). Ensure that you keep Exercise Sheet 10 with you at all times. If you do drink, record and challenge your permissive thoughts as soon as possible after they have occurred. If you engage in this exercise on a regular basis you should find that as your belief in the permissive thoughts decreases so will your desire to keep on drinking when a drinking episode starts.

As with tackling uncontrollability thoughts, don't become dejected if progress is not swift. And don't expect too much too soon. It takes time to generate and strengthen your belief in alternative thoughts. Beware also of the 'yes . . . but' thoughts that lurk around. You know how they can get in the way of progress. Try and challenge these thoughts with the eight key questions listed above. You will need to repeat this process until your 'yes . . . but' thoughts are reduced.

CHAPTER SUMMARY

- It is fundamental to identify permissive thoughts at the time they occur.
- Once permissive thoughts are identified it is important to learn to challenge them.
- Identifying and challenging permissive thoughts will take effort and practice.
- If you engage in identifying and challenging permissive thoughts on a regular basis, you should find that, as your belief in the permissive thoughts decreases, your desire to keep on drinking when a drinking episode starts will also decrease.

9

Challenging positive thoughts about drinking

Positive thoughts about drinking are important because they can help trigger drinking episodes. In this chapter, we will look at how to identify and challenge these thoughts. Some typical positive thoughts will include:

- Drinking makes me more affectionate.
- Drinking helps me to control negative thoughts.
- Drinking reduces my anxious feelings.
- Drinking makes me more sociable.
- Drinking helps me fit in socially.
- Drinking reduces my self-consciousness.

Exercise 11 will help you identify your positive thoughts about drinking. By now these exercises should feel fairly familiar! An example of a completed exercise follows.

EXERCISE 11

1 Write down the activating event of your drinking episode. Run through the questions at the bottom of the table under the heading 'Activating event'.

2 Under the heading 'Feelings and sensations' write down the feelings (e.g. anxiety, sadness, worry) and sensations you noticed before the drinking escalated.

3 Under the heading 'Positive thoughts' write down all the thoughts you had before the drinking started. Make sure you identify the key thought (the thought that most increases the probability that you will start drinking) and highlight it. Practice doing this exercise whenever possible over the next month. Don't forget that practice will make it easier to identify these thoughts.

As with permissive thoughts, it is important to learn and practice how to challenge positive thoughts. You should always ask yourself these eight key questions when challenging positive thoughts:

1 Do these thoughts make it easier or harder to drink?
2 What would I say to someone else?
3 What have I learned from drinking in the past that could help me now?
4 Am I being misled by my feelings?
5 What are the consequences of thinking in this way?
6 How will I feel later?
7 What would someone else say about this thought?
8 Is this situation similar to past situations?

EXERCISE 11: EXAMPLE
IDENTIFYING POSITIVE THOUGHTS ABOUT DRINKING

Activating event	Feelings and sensations	Positive thoughts
Coming back from work, seeing the house empty and thinking of an argument I had at work.	Angry and low.	I will feel better after a drink. Drinking will make me control negative thoughts.
At a party, meeting new people.	Anxious.	Drinking will make me more sociable. Drinking will make me fit in.
On a Friday afternoon, at a conference, I asked a poor question.	Anxious and angry.	Alcohol is the only way to get rid of the anxiety and anger.
On a Saturday afternoon, I was walking along a canal.	Bored and frustrated.	The only way I'll have fun today is if I drink.

EXERCISE 11
IDENTIFYING POSITIVE THOUGHTS ABOUT DRINKING

Activating event	Feelings and sensations	Positive thoughts
When did it happen? Where were you? What were you doing? What were you thinking about?	What feelings and body sensations did you notice?	How did you think drinking would help? What were you afraid might happen if you did not drink?

This exercise can be extended to include additional information for challenging the positive thoughts you have been noting down. Exercise 12 follows the same format used for challenging permissive thoughts. An example of completed exercise follows.

EXERCISE 12

1 Write down the activating event of your drinking episode, the associated feelings and sensations, and the positive thoughts. Identify the key positive thought and highlight it.
2 Under the heading 'Evidence not supporting the thought' write down all the evidence that suggests that the thought is not true. Use the eight questions for challenging positive thoughts listed above.
3 Under the heading 'Alternative thought' record an alternative and more balanced thought. Again, use the eight questions for challenging positive thoughts.
4 Rate how much you believe the alternative thought to be true on a scale of 0–100 per cent.

It is important to challenge your thoughts as often as you can. Ensure that you keep Exercise Sheet 12 with you at all times. If you do drink, record and challenge your positive thoughts as soon as possible after they have occurred. If you engage in this exercise on a regular basis you will find that as your belief in the positive thoughts decreases so will your desire to start drinking.

Remember not to become dejected if progress is not swift. As with the previous exercises, beware of expecting too much and too soon as it takes time to generate and believe

EXERCISE 12: EXAMPLE
RECOGNIZING AND CHALLENGING POSITIVE THOUGHTS ABOUT DRINKING

Activating event	Feelings and sensation	Positive thoughts	Evidence not supporting the thought	Alternative thought	Belief in alternative thought
Coming back from work, seeing the house empty and thinking of an argument I had at work.	Angry and low.	I will feel better after a drink.	The good feeling does not last that long.	I will feel so bad after drinking that it is better to avoid it!	95%
		Drinking will make me control negative thoughts.	They still come back, usually much worse, after I've been drinking.	Drinking worsens my negative thoughts.	95%
At a party, meeting new new people.	Anxious.	Drinking will make me more sociable.	I get aggressive when I drink, which ends up ruining my evenings.	Drinking might make me relaxed, but it won't last for long and usually results in a mess.	85%
On a Friday afternoon, at a conference, I asked a poor question.	Anxious and angry.	Drinking will make me fit in.	The anxiety or anger will go without me having to start drinking. There are positive things I can do to speed up this up (e.g. talk to someone but not about my drinking).	The anxiety and anger will go and I can help this along. Alcohol will make me feel worse not better. I need to break the pattern of coping with negative emotions by using alcohol. It leads to cycles of disruption and distress.	98%

On a Saturday afternoon, I was walking along a canal.	Bored and frustrated	The only way I'll have fun today is if I drink.	In the past, I have tolerated days where I've felt bored.	Everyone has the odd 'boring' day from time to time. I can put up with feeling bored today. I might not need to. Do something positive. I may have some fun.	95%
		Alcohol is the only way to get rid of the anxiety and anger.	Drinking will make my emotional state worse rather than better. It would result in drunkenness and bad behavior; tomorrow, I'd hate myself and feel depressed.		
			There are things I can do that don't involve alcohol, which will probably be fun or interesting (e.g. cinema or meet friends for coffee and chat).		
			Drinking to cope with negative emotions (as I well know) leads to cycles of distress and disruption.		

EXERCISE 12
RECOGNIZING AND CHALLENGING POSITIVE THOUGHTS ABOUT DRINKING

Activating event	Feelings and sensation	Positive thoughts	Evidence not supporting the thought	Alternative thought	Belief in alternative thought
When did it happen? Where were you? What were you doing? What are you thinking about?	What feelings and body sensations did you notice?	What were you saying to yourself that made it easier to keep drinking? Highlight the key thought that makes it most likely to continue drinking.	Use the eight questions above to challenge your thought.	Note the alternative more helpful thought.	Rate how much you believe this thought to be true on a scale of 0–100%.

in alternative thoughts. Keep an eye on the 'yes . . . but' thoughts. Always try to challenge these with the eight key questions listed above. You will need to repeat this process until your 'yes . . . but' thoughts are reduced.

CHAPTER SUMMARY

- It is fundamental to identify positive thoughts at the time they occur.
- Once positive thoughts are identified it is important to learn to challenge them.
- Identifying and challenging positive thoughts will take effort and practice.
- If you engage in identifying and challenging positive thoughts on a regular basis you should find that as your belief in the positive thoughts decreases your desire to start drinking will also decrease.

10

Tackling craving

Craving can be described as a subjective sense of *desiring* to attain the state induced by drinking. This desire is usually a mixture of physical and emotional arousal, thoughts and memories. It is almost inevitable that when you stop or reduce your drinking there will be times when you will experience craving. This is fine, so long as you don't act on it. Craving will abate *naturally* if unfulfilled and, over time, you will recognize that it is *controllable* and that there are a variety of ways to deal with it.

It is useful to think of craving just as a signal to *take action*. The purpose of this chapter is to help you develop skills to identify the types of situations or events that can trigger craving, the thoughts that may be unhelpful in these situations, and some techniques to steady yourself so you don't slip.

The typical situations that may trigger craving will include:

The environment

Triggers associated with drinking are a major source of craving. These will include the sight of alcohol or a pub, seeing other people drink and time cues (e.g. a certain time of the day and/or a day in the week).

Memories of the drinking life

Sometimes you may find yourself thinking of your drinking as a long-lost friend or partner and have thoughts such as: 'A cold beer really tasted good,' 'I remember how good it felt when I used to drink a few cold beers on a lovely summer evening,' or 'What's going out in the evening without a drink?'.

Negative emotions

When you experience unpleasant thoughts or feelings, or when you are bored or stressed and find it hard to iden-tify ways of enjoying yourself, you are more likely to expe-rience craving. Typically at these times you may think: 'I need a drink right now. When this is all over I will stop again'.

Wanting to enhance a positive experience

Sometimes you may experience the onset of craving when you wish to enhance a positive experience. For example you may have learned to associate drinking with social-izing and think that drinking will make social interactions more 'enjoyable' and 'spontaneous'.

Challenging uncontrollability thoughts about craving

By now you should be proficient in identifying and challenging a variety of unhelpful thoughts, including uncontrollability, permissive and positive thoughts about drinking. The same principles we used for identifying and challeng-ing these thoughts can be applied to un-controllability thoughts about craving. Examples of these types of thoughts typically include:

- Craving is a physical reaction, so I cannot do anything about it.
- Craving will make me go crazy.
- I cannot control my craving.

If you believe that you cannot control your craving or that your craving will make you go crazy you will probably have good reasons for it! In the past you may have struggled with craving and/or ended up drinking to relieve it. Exercise 13 will help you identify what it is that makes you think you cannot control your craving. An example of a completed exercise follows.

EXERCISE 13

1 At the top of Exercise Sheet 13 write down typical uncontrollability thoughts you experience about your craving. Try to use your own words as far as possible.

EXERCISE 13: JOANNE
EVIDENCE FOR AND AGAINST UNCONTROLLABILITY OF CRAVING

Craving thoughts	Belief in each thought (0–100%)
(a) Craving is a physical reaction, so I cannot do anything about it.	90%
(b) When I am craving alcohol I cannot function.	90%
(c) A craving will go on and on, making drinking inevitable.	90%
(d) Cravings will keep coming back and they'll make me drink eventually.	90%

Evidence for	Evidence against
(a) I get a terrible craving in the evening, and the only way to deal with it is to drink because it's the body needing the alcohol.	(a) There are many reasons that can trigger craving that are to do with the environment rather than what my body feels like. Sometimes I managed not to act on my craving when I was not at home or when I was distracted.
(b) I cannot seem to concentrate on anything when I am craving alcohol. It takes up all my head space.	(b) At times, I have managed to go to work, be with friends and play sports when I was craving. This actually helped me to deal with it and I found it did not last forever.
(c) I've had one craving in the past that lasted for four or five days, and which culminated in drinking.	(c) I recently had a craving that lasted for two or three days. But I didn't start drinking and it eventually disappeared.
(d) I still get cravings from time to time.	(d) The cravings I have now are relatively infrequent, mild and last only for an hour or two. I haven't started drinking because of them.

Things have changed in my life, since starting CBT, which has resulted in fewer cravings, milder cravings, and much higher levels of motivation and commitment to stay abstinent.

Outcome

With commitment I can control my craving. Experience suggests that it is not an entirely physical reaction but has much to do with where I am and what I am doing. If I experience a craving I can probably try to do those things that worked out in the past, such as concentrate on work or get distracted. Craving does not last forever! The more attention I pay to it the worse it becomes. I have resisted even severe craving, I can do it again. I know what to do. I need high levels of motivation and commitment to stay abstinent. Craving now is infrequent and usually mild and short-lived. Such craving isn't a big problem.

Rerating of belief in each thought (0–10%)

(a) Craving is a physical reaction, so I cannot do anything about it. (10%)
(b) When I am craving alcohol I cannot function. (10%)
(c) A craving will go on and on, making drinking inevitable. (10%)
(d) Cravings will keep coming back and I'll drink on one eventually. (10%)

EXERCISE 13
EVIDENCE FOR AND AGAINST THE UNCONTROLLABILITY OF CRAVING

Craving thoughts	Belief in each thought (0–100%)

Evidence for	Evidence against

Outcome

Rerating of belief in each thought (0–100%)

2 Rate your belief in each thought on a scale of 0–100 per cent.

3 At this point you have to ask yourself what evidence there is for and against your thoughts about craving. Typical evidence may include:

- Drinking every time you experience craving
- Not being able to do anything else when you experience craving.
- Behaving in a crazed way when you have a craving.

Ensure that you make a list of all this evidence under the heading 'Evidence for'. The next step is to examine this evidence more carefully. You may be misinterpreting the evidence relevant to your craving. The questions you have to ask yourself to challenge the evidence for lack of control over craving are:

- Is the evidence for lack of control over my craving true 100 per cent of the time?
- Is there evidence that it might not be true 100 per cent of the time?
- Do I really drink every time I have a craving?
- Have there been times when I have not experienced craving in a craving-inducing situation?
- Can I recall one episode when my craving stopped once it had started?
- Have there been times when I could have given into my craving and did not?

Make sure you challenge and re-interpret one piece of evidence at a time.

4 At this stage begin to consider what the evidence suggests. Write a brief summary of your conclusions under the heading 'Outcome'. After you have done this rerate how much you believe in your initial thoughts. Take a look at the completed Exercise Sheet to help you.

By now you will have probably realized that some of your uncontrollability thoughts about craving may not be completely grounded in evidence. Despite this, you may still have doubts that you can have some control over your craving. This is because you are likely to have some reservations about the *new thought* that you *can* control your craving. These reservations are natural and are typically expressed in the form of the now familiar 'yes . . . but' sentences. A typical example would be: '*Yes*, I know I can control my craving, *but* only when I am alone.'

Giving up thoughts about craving will not be easy. After all, there is a good reason why they are there. The reason is the same as the reasons underpinning all other sets of thoughts that we discussed. Thoughts about the uncontrollability of craving take away *responsibility* from you. A very important part of successfully tackling your craving will be accepting that you are responsible for what you do and that you can do things differently if you so wish. Hopefully the final exercises in this chapter will help you strengthen the belief that you do have some control over your craving. Make sure you carry out the exercise or exercises that will work for you. This will entail trial and error. Don't be discouraged if it does not always work for you. As with all the techniques in this book repeated practice is key for success!

Techniques to deal with craving

Coping statements

When craving is strong you may find it difficult to reason objectively. Generating coping statements can be helpful to get you through a critical period. The following are examples of coping statements:

- I will put up a fight.
- I'll feel healthy and remorse-free in the morning.
- Get the hell out of the situation now!
- I can spend money saved on gigs, CDs, visits, or clothes.
- I'll be breaking negative patterns of behavior sooner rather than later, and be making life easier for myself.
- I'll be taking responsibility for myself and my future.

Try and think of examples of coping statements that might help you in critical situations and write them down.

Distraction

The key goal of this technique is to get you to shift the focus of your attention from internal triggers (e.g. moods, thoughts, memories and physical sensations) to the external environment. Some strategies you can adopt include:

- *Describing your surroundings*. Describe anything that takes your fancy (e.g. shop fronts, cars, monuments, people). You should attempt to go into as much detail as possible with your descriptions.
- *Talking*. This may involve starting a conversation with a friend, a colleague or a family member.

- *Trigger avoidance*. You can remove yourself from cue-laden environments (e.g. a pub, people drinking) by, for example, taking a brisk walk, visiting a friend or going for a drive.
- *Household chores*. Performing household chores will not only serve as a distraction but will also help you boost your self-esteem because you have accomplished something useful.
- *Games*. You may want to spend time involved in games, such as board games, video games, cards or puzzles. These activities can be quite challenging and will require concentration. In addition, you will be able to engage in some of them by yourself.

Image replacement

It is commonplace, especially after a few weeks of abstinence or reduced drinking, to have pictures or dreams of oneself drinking. In these images drinking is usually perceived as a method for coping with distress. It is helpful to substitute the positive image with a negative image regarding the damaging consequences of drinking. These may include feeling hopeless and anxious, losing money, jobs and partners. If this image replacement technique causes distress you may want to replace the positive image of drinking with a positive image regarding the benefits of not drinking. These may include being back at work again, having more money, being better able to take care of your children and so on.

Review the benefits of not drinking and the costs of drinking

Thoughts about the positive consequences of not drinking and the costs of drinking will weaken cravings. Make your own personal list of both from the material developed in the earlier chapters.

Decisional delay

When you have a strong craving, put off the decision to drink for 20 minutes. Cravings usually go or weaken substantially if you do not drink for this period of time. Remind yourself that craving will not last indefinitely.

Developing a flashcard

You can sum up all the information on managing your craving on a flashcard. This will be of invaluable use when craving occurs and you need to tackle it quickly and effectively. An example of completed flashcard is shown in Figure 10.1.

What happens if things do not work out?

There is no need to panic if the exercises sometimes go wrong. As discussed earlier this is likely to happen, especially at the beginning, when you are still practising how to carry them out. Negative and positive outcomes are equally useful as they are part of the 'relearning' process. Setbacks are simply an indication that a closer look at your strategy is needed to ensure that you carry out the revised

MANAGING MY CRAVING

Distraction: (a) describe surroundings; (b) phone friend but don't talk about craving; (c) do chores; or (d) learn a poem or do a puzzle.

Coping statements: 'Put up a fight'; 'I'll feel healthy and remorse-free in the morning'; 'I'll avoid unwanted, dangerous, expensive behavior'; 'I can spend money saved on gigs, CDs, visits or clothes'; 'I'll not be creating financial, occupational, or emotional problems for myself'; 'I'll be breaking negative patterns of behavior sooner rather than later, and be making life easier for myself'; and 'I'll be taking responsibility for myself and my future'.

Visual images: (a) replace a cosy drinking image with a negative drinking image (e.g. puking up in the street; being somewhere or doing something I'll regret; nasty memory; head buried in the pillow; going to buy booze in the morning); (b) an image of myself as strong, while crushing, in one hand, a pint of beer or bottle of wine.

Figure 10.1 An example of a craving flashcard

exercises utilizing what you have learned. In order to do this you will need to pinpoint what the problem was. The key questions to ask yourself, as usual, are:

- Was the exercise too difficult?
- Are my expectations too high?
- What thoughts did I have?
- What did I learn from this?
- What can I do differently?

CHAPTER SUMMARY

- Uncontrollability thoughts are very important in craving.
- The common type of evidence for uncontrollability involves thinking that your craving will bring you to drink all the time and on every occasion.
- You probably have evidence that you cannot control your craving, as well as that you can.
- You need to become conscious of the fact that you do have some degree of control over your craving and that you are responsible for choosing to act on it or not.
- A variety of exercises can be employed to confirm and strengthen your sense of control over craving. Remember that a negative outcome is just as useful as a positive one and a necessary step for change.

11

Identifying apparently irrelevant decisions

During the course of the day you make thousands of decisions. Some of the smaller and more ordinary ones appear to have nothing to do with drinking. In reality, it may be these smaller and more ordinary decisions that *cumulatively* bring you to a point at which drinking becomes very probable. It is hard to recognize, when you are in the midst of the decision-making process, that you may be heading in the wrong direction. This is because so many choices do not appear to involve drinking at the time you are considering them.

One of the best things to do is to try to think about every decision you have to make, irrespective of how apparently irrelevant it is to drinking. This will involve thinking ahead about every possible option and anticipating high-risk situations. At first this may feel awkward, but after some time it will become an automatic process.

The first step is to *identify an apparently irrelevant decision* you made that resulted in a slip. Think of a time, in the recent past, when you had a slip after a period of abstinence. Ask yourself the following questions:

DECISION SHEET 1 (PAST SLIPS): JOANNE

Preceding event/ situation	Apparently irrelevant decision	What could have been done differently	Pros of doing things differently	Cons of doing things differently	Safe alternative
Early evening. Working poorly. Felt low and frustrated. Recently found out ex-boyfriend has new girlfriend.	Aimlessly walking around central London, on my own.	Done some focused activity that would have given me pleasure (e.g. cinema, running).	Would have taken mind off work and boyfriend, and improved my mood.		Visit cinema or go running.
Morning. In bed. Felt low and angry.	Lay in bed for most of the day.	(a) Got up and immediately done something enjoyable and positive (e.g. running). (b) Had a manageable plan for the day that included things to look forward to.	(a) Would have 'stopped the rot' and lifted my mood. (b) Manageable plan would have increased likelihood of getting out of bed and made me feel better about the day, esp. if plan included pleasurable activities.		Get up and go running. Have plan for day that's manageable, not overwhelming, and includes activities to look forward to.
Lying in bed during the day.	Visualized drink and drug experiences.	Get out of bed. Replace 'positive' drinking images with negative realistic images. Do something distracting (e.g. novel, watch a film).	Would have taken my focus away from craving-inducing images, and reduced craving.		Replace 'positive' drinking images with negative realistic ones. Do something distracting (e.g. novel, watch a film).

DECISION SHEET 2					
Preceding event/ situation	Apparently irrelevant decision	What could have been done differently	Pros of doing things differently	Cons of doing things differently	Safe alternative

- What events and/or situation preceded the slip?
- Who was I with?
- Where was I and what day, time and week was it?
- What decisions led to the slip?
- What could I have done differently?
- What are the pros and cons of doing things differently?
- What will I do next time – what is the safe alternative?

Examples of apparently irrelevant decisions that may lead to a slip can include:

- Not making plans for the weekend.
- Keeping alcohol at home.
- Going to a party where people are drinking.
- Going to the pub to see old drinking pals.

Use the Decision Sheet above for this exercise. An example of a completed sheet can be found in Decision Sheet 1. Identify as many apparently irrelevant decisions you can.

Once you have done this, repeat the exercise with any

DECISION SHEET 3 (UPCOMING DECISIONS): JOANNE					
Preceding event/ situation	Apparently irrelevant decision	What could have been done differently	Pros of doing things differently	Cons of doing things differently	Safe alternative
My boss has invited me to his wedding reception on 25 June.	(Done) Accepted invitation.	Decline invitation.	Avoid a risky situation.	It wouldn't be nice to miss his wedding reception.	Rehearse drinking refusal skills. Review motivation exercises. Leave early.
Parents have asked me to go on holiday with them and brother during winter break.	(Option) Decline offer.	N/A	Avoid risky situation.	Greatly disappoint parents.	Discuss with a friend. Accept, but, prior to holiday, fortify myself (i.e. plan things to do on holiday, rehearse drinking refusal skill, and review my exercises).
	(Option) Accept offer.	N/A	Please parents and good for family.	Committed to risky situation without having thought things through.	

apparently irrelevant *upcoming* decision that you think may lead to drinking. An example of this can be found in Decision Sheet 3. Remember that decisions may involve any aspect of your life, such as friends, recreational activities, family or work. When faced with a high-risk option you should *generally* choose a safe alternative. On the other hand you might, for some reason, decide on a high-risk option. If so, ensure that you plan how to protect yourself in the high-risk situation. An example would be stopping at a pub where you used to go drinking but only after having well rehearsed drinking refusal skills and being highly motivated to change. It is easier to avoid the high-risk situation than to resist temptation once you are in the middle of it.

CHAPTER SUMMARY

- Apparently irrelevant decisions may cumulatively bring you to a point at which drinking becomes very probable.
- By learning to identify apparently irrelevant decisions you can cut the chances of drinking slips.

12

Focusing on key skills

In this chapter we will focus on four sets of skills that are key in helping you cope with high-risk situations that commonly precipitate a drinking episode: refusing drinks, receiving criticisms about drinking, problem-solving, and general assertiveness. You may have been drinking for a long time but never adequately developed or strengthened these skills; or you may possess adequate skills that have fallen into disuse. Focusing on these skills will, therefore, contain much that is novel or provide a much needed review.

Refusing drinks

It is inevitable that people around you will offer you drinks or pressure you to drink. This is a high-risk situation to be in if you have decided to stop or reduce your drinking. Family gatherings, office parties, dates, dinners with friends are some of the settings in which alcohol will be encountered. Fellow workers, relatives and dates might offer you a drink without knowing your drinking history. This might range from a single casual offer of a drink to fully fledged pressure to drink. Being able to say no to a drink will require more than a commitment to stop drinking. Specific assertiveness skills will be necessary. These will allow you to respond more effectively to real situations when they arise.

Voice and eye contact

Refuse the drink in an unhesitant manner. Your voice will have to be clear and firm. This should be done so as to prevent questioning about whether you mean what you say. Ensure that you make direct eye contact with the other person as it will increase the effectiveness of the message.

Change subject of conversation and suggest an alternative

After refusing the drink, change the subject of conversation so as to avoid being drawn into a debate about drinking. You may also want to do something else, such as go for a walk or a drive or suggest something else to drink or eat (coffee, dessert).

Ask for a change in behavior

If the person continues to pressure you, clarify that you do not want him or her to offer you a drink. For example 'Thanks for offering me a drink, but I just don't want it, so please stop asking me.'

Avoid excuses and vague answers

'I don't feel that well' or 'I would usually have one, but not tonight' will only serve to postpone having to face refusing a drink. It might also imply that at some later date you will accept a drink, putting more pressure on yourself and the person offering it. However, in extreme cases excuses may be a last resort.

Rehearse

You should try to rehearse your drinking refusal skills ahead of encountering any high-risk situation. In the example below a client prepared himself ahead of a wedding reception, where he knew he would inevitably be offered a drink.

Wedding guest: *Would you like a drink?*

Me: *I'll have a coke, please.*

Wedding guest: *Come on. Just one drink! It's an important day! Don't spoil it by being boring!*

Me: *I'm not drinking at the moment.*

Wedding guest: *Why not?*

Me: *Drinking doesn't agree with me.*

Wedding guest: *Why doesn't it agree with you?*

Me: *There are plenty of other things we can talk about. Please stop bothering me about drinking and let's talk about something else.*

Receiving criticism about drinking

In day-to-day life we are bound to stumble across critical statements. If criticism is delivered properly, it can actually provide us with a chance to learn valuable things about ourselves and how we affect others. If it is not, it may lead to communication breakdown and fighting. Our inability to respond effectively to criticism can also trigger critical interpersonal conflicts, whereas an effective response can minimize conflicts and, consequently, the probability of drinking. One of the most difficult things to do in our exchanges with others is to learn to interpret any criticism we receive in a benign manner, ensuring that we focus on separating our *emotions* about the criticism from the *information* presented in the criticism.

Problem drinking may have affected your life in a variety of ways making you susceptible to a variety of criticisms about your behavior. So it is especially important that you are able to respond to criticism in a constructive way. Criticism can be either *destructive* or *constructive*. Neither warrants an emotional or hostile reaction to it. Destructive criticism arises when someone criticizes *you as a person*, rather than criticizing *your behavior*. The intention of this form of criticism may be to hurt: this type of criticism is often linked to the other person's emotional state or may be a provocation to fight. The use of the words 'always' or 'never' features prominently in destructive criticism:

- *You are always home late. You will never stop drinking!*

Constructive criticism targets behavior, not the person. The other person attempts to describe his or her feelings with regard to your behavior and usually asks you to change in some way:

- *I worry when you are late coming home. I start thinking you may be on a binge. Could you let me know you are OK?*

Criticism can take many forms. A typical one regards *slips* ('Here we go again. You went out with Joe . . . you are drinking again!'). You will find that, even if you are committed to stop drinking, it may take time for others in your life to increase trust and to diminish their own excessive vigilance about recurrence of drinking episodes. Sometimes this criticism is unfounded, sometimes it may not be. In both cases it is important to respond in a way that fosters constructive communication rather than fighting. At times, criticism will focus on *past drinking* ('I hated you when you were drinking, you destroyed our family'). It is important to avoid dwelling on the past and use your resources on focusing on the here-and-now solutions. During the initial period of sobriety, criticism about drinking may be accompanied by criticisms about other behaviors of yours. For example, your partner may be upset about your low mood and desire to be alone. However, instead of directly addressing these behaviors, he or she may avoid mentioning them and focus instead on the present risk of drinking or past drinking behavior. This unfounded criticism may occur because drinking has been associated with these other behaviors of yours in the past (you may have started drinking when your mood was low) or because criticizing drinking has become an automatic process. Again, irrespective of how the criticism is phrased, it is crucial to be able to clarify the person's real concerns.

This will not occur unless you can respond adequately to the initial criticism and thus avoid getting diverted into a fight or an argument.

The following tips are aimed at improving your ability to receive criticism (irrespective of whether it is constructive or destructive) and understanding important information contained in the criticism.

Avoid counter-attack

Getting defensive and responding with your own criticisms will only fuel the argument, preventing effective communication from taking place.

Get more information

Find out more about the criticism in question. This will encourage straightforward statements about your behavior which are more likely to improve communication. For example, if your partner criticizes you for wanting to spend time on a new hobby, a non-confrontational (a reply uttered in a calm tone of voice) could be something on the lines of 'I cannot figure out what is it about my hobby that aggravates you. Could you tell me?'

Agree on something and restate it in a clearer way

Instead of responding aggressively, we can accept those negative things that are said about us that are true. For example, if you have not been drinking but your partner says:

You always come home late. You will never stop drinking!

You might reply by saying:

You are right; I often come home late. This is because of my job, but I understand why you are concerned because when I used to drink I always used to come home late, too.

In this reply part of the initial statement that was right ('You are always late.') is validated. The part of the statement which relates to the partner's concern and is expressed destructively ('You will never stop drinking!') is *restated*. This takes away the negativity and confrontation element of the initial statement, allowing the partner to respond more objectively.

Compromise

This entails proposing some behavioral change as a response to the criticism. In this case it may mean ensuring that some days during the week you are home early.

Problem-solving

We can all find ourselves confronted by difficult situations. However, a situation can become a problem if a person has no effective means of coping with it. Difficult situations may arise as a result of dealings with other people and from our own thoughts and negative emotions. Effective problem-solving necessitates recognizing that you are facing a problem situation and resisting the appeal of either doing nothing or responding precipitately. Generating an effective solution will require that you pause to assess the situation in order to be able to decide which actions will be in your interest. If you don't identify a good solution to the problem it will escalate over time. This may, in turn, act as a trigger for drinking. Problem-solving skills are thus a necessary component for tackling problem drinking effectively, since any problem can straightforwardly set the stage for a slip. The following tips are aimed at improving your ability to deal with problems as they arise.

Recognizing the problem

The first, and most important, task is to identify whether there is a problem. Some of the clues that usually indicate the presence of a problem include: physical sensations (craving, indigestion, palpitations), thoughts and feelings (particularly worry, but also anxiety, low mood, anger and many other emotions), behavior (neglecting your appearance, poor work performance) and interaction with people (they criticize you, you avoid them).

Having recognized that something might be wrong, attempt to define the problem as precisely as possible. This will entail gathering information, but only information based on hard facts. Break down the problem into small parts as you will find it easier to manage each part rather than confronting the problem as a whole. For example, an imminent party might give rise to the following concern:

- *I have to attend Joe's birthday party in a fortnight and be friendly with Caroline.*

This concern reflects two sub-problems:

1 *I have to deal with being anxious at meeting people and being offered a drink.*
2 *I have to see my ex-girlfriend Caroline and be polite to her.*

Generating solutions

It is important to generate a number of solutions to any given problem, because the first one that comes to mind may not be the most appropriate. Several approaches can help you identify possible solutions:

- *Mindstorming.* When you mindstorm you generate solutions without evaluating whether they are good or not. It is best to write them down on a piece of paper as they come, so that you can reconsider them once the process is over.
- *Past solutions.* You may be able to think of a solution that worked before, or ask someone else about solutions that have worked for them in the past. It is likely that an 'old' solution will have to be 'tailored' to fit your present needs.
- *Reframing.* It may be of help to take a step back from the situation. How would you advise a friend if they had the same problem you did?

Solutions to 'I have to attend Joe's birthday party in a fortnight . . . ' might include:

- Send my apologies.
- Have a drink in order to calm down.
- Recall how I coped last time.
- Talk about my anxiety with a friend.

Evaluating the pros and cons of the solutions

Once you have generated solutions, you will need to evaluate the pros and cons of each in order to decide which will have to be rejected because of its unsuitability.

- Send my apologies: *reject*, as it is Joe's 40th birthday.
- Have a drink in order to calm down: *reject*, as I am not drinking now.
- Recall how I coped last time: *accept*, as I did quite well at a party a week ago and successfully refused drinks that I was offered.
- Talk about my anxiety with a friend: *accept*, as some of my friends can be supportive.

Choosing a solution

Following this you will have to rank the solutions according to their usefulness for you at this time:

1st solution: Recall how I coped last time.
2nd solution: Talk about my anxiety with a friend.

Planning to implement the solution

Once you have done this, take your first choice solution and start planning how to put it into action. Make sure you answer the following questions:

- What will I do?
- How will I do it?
- When will it be done?
- Who will be involved?
- What is my back-up plan?

The problem-solving action would entail recalling how you coped last time and answering the above questions one by one, for example:

- Find a place where I will not be disturbed.
- Recall all the details of the last party and write down all the strategies I remember using to help me get through the evening.
- Immediately, as the party is tonight.
- Me.
- If I cannot remember I will try the 2nd solution.

Whenever possible, try to rehearse dealing with your task (in this example going to the birthday party) either by imagining it or by role playing with someone you know. Make sure you scan your solutions to see if you could combine them. For example, you may find that asking your friend to rehearse with you will allow you to solve this problem more effectively.

Implementing the solution and evaluating your performance

Implement your solution and review whether it is successful or not. If it is, congratulate yourself and remember what you did for the future. If it is not, try to understand what went wrong. Perhaps that day you were not feeling great, you may have been over-ambitious or have misjudged something. As with everything in life, learn as much as you can from the experience, go back to the original solution list and start by selecting the next option. Don't forget that the more solutions you generate the greater the chances are of solving the problem!

General assertiveness

Assertiveness is a very effective way of letting others know what is going on with you, as well as what effect their behavior has on you. Being assertive frequently results in correcting a problem that is at the source of stress and tension, which, if not dealt with properly, may lead to problem drinking. Acting assertively will thus decrease the chances of using alcohol inappropriately as well as improve the quality of your life.

Being *assertive* means:

- being able to recognize your rights and the rights of others
- being able to clearly state your feelings and needs
- being aware of what you want and what you don't want and acting accordingly
- being able to confront difficult situations head-on instead of being intimidated, afraid, aggressive or manipulative.

Now, compare assertiveness with aggression and passivity.

- An aggressive interpersonal style is characterized by:
  - imposing your needs and feelings on others
  - running over others' rights while protecting your own
  - attempting to achieve your goals even when others are hurt or treated unfairly.
- A passive interpersonal style is characterized by:
  - failing to communicate your needs and feelings
  - giving up your rights to avoid conflict
  - always wanting to please others.

Assertive people will occasionally act in a passive way (e.g. with an insensitive boss) and can also respond aggressively (e.g. with someone who is pushy). Assertive people are free to be who they are and are more likely to have their needs met. They also tend to experience less interpersonal stress and have better social relationships. Learning how to assert yourself is an essential step in your claim to personal happiness and well-being.

Common misconception

'You are either assertive or not. You can't learn it.' Everybody can learn to be assertive. It is not a personality trait, unchangeable and fixed. Some people are always aware of what feels right for them. Others are almost always confused. The majority of people are somewhere in between: assertive in some situations, and non-assertive in others. These last two groups can benefit from learning to be assertive more often.

TIPS

Becoming more assertive involves a number of steps:
- *Think before you speak.* Decide in advance what you want and what is fair. Prepare yourself:
  - Think about your request ('I want to discuss . . . with you').
  - Your feelings ('I feel . . . about the situation').
  - Your needs ('I would appreciate you doing . . . about this situation').

- *Question your assumptions about other people's intentions.* Are you being objective and rational? Discuss it with somebody if you are unsure. Write things down, as this helps clarify your thoughts. Have a contingency plan for coping if things do not go smoothly.
- *Ask for what you want clearly.* Be brief and specific. Avoid rambling on about the same point. State your needs in a factual manner and wait for a response. Avoid side-tracking and theorizing. Practice how you are going to state your needs beforehand if necessary.
- *Be aware of your body language.* Posture is important. Stand tall. Respect personal space. Maintain eye contact as it shows sincerity, confidence and interest. Avoid fidgeting. Facial expression and tone of voice should match message.
- *Listen to what the other person has to say about your request.* Be sure you understand their point of view and ask for clarifications if you don't. Be willing to compromise. Restate your assertion if you feel you are not being heard.

Common difficulties

Sometimes, you may get too emotional about an issue, because you are nervous and doubtful or aggressive. Try to remain calm by maintaining relaxed posture and applying deep breathing (see Appendix 1 for relaxation techniques). After you've stated your needs, shift your attention to the other person and *listen* to what they have to say, rather than keeping your attention on yourself, and *look out for* signs of their discomfort.

It is hard to put this into practice. It is not easy to change your interpersonal style, nor will it happen overnight. It can also be quite frightening to assert yourself especially if you have adopted a passive style for a number of years. Try to change things gradually. Make a list of things you want to change and work from the bottom of the list, the easiest things first. Once you've achieved these, you can slowly work upwards, leaving the hardest challenges at the end. Reward yourself when you've achieved something. Over time, your confidence will grow and you will start reaping the benefits of being able to assert your rights and needs.

CHAPTER SUMMARY

- When refusing a drink remember to do so in an unhesitant manner. If necessary, change the subject of conversation and suggest alternative activities. If the person continues to pressure you, be firm in clarifying that you do not want a drink. Remember to avoid excuses as they will end up piling the pressure to drink.

- When receiving criticism about drinking remember to separate emotions about the criticism from the information presented in the criticism, irrespective of whether the criticism is constructive or destructive.

- There are four key steps to take in dealing with criticism about drinking: avoid counter-attack, get more information, agree on something and restate it in a clearer way, and compromise.

- When you have a problem, you can tackle it through problem-solving. This involves seven steps: recognizing the problem, generating solutions, evaluating the pros and cons of the solutions, choosing a solution, planning to implement the solution, implementing it, and evaluating your performance. Remember that if your chosen solution does not work you will have to choose another one from your list and repeat the process.

- Building general assertiveness skills will increase the chances of dealing with problems that are at the source of stress and tension. The same stress and tension that, if not dealt with properly, may lead to problem drinking. Acting assertively will thus decrease the chances of using alcohol inappropriately as well as improve the quality of your life.

13

Increasing pleasurable activities

As discussed earlier, it is inevitable that you will experience concerns about giving up or changing your drinking behavior – most, if not all people, do. One of the most common concerns is that stopping drinking or changing your drinking patterns will expose a *void* in your life. This may well be the case if you have a life composed of eating, sleeping, working and drinking, as dropping the latter activity would only leave you with eating, sleeping and working. Not the most exciting of combinations! In this case, giving up drinking would entail giving up a large chunk of your recreation time, social activities, friends and past ways of having fun. In other words, key sources of pleasure. The absence of these sources of pleasure may well end up exacerbating any negative emotions you may be feeling (such as boredom, anxiety, worry, depression) which, in turn, will increase the chances of wanting the quick fix of a drink. So it is of paramount importance to engage in alternative pleasurable activities when you stop or reduce your drinking, as these will bring an improvement in mood and a reduction in the probability of slipping.

Most people present little or no difficulties in shifting

their thoughts to other matters or in filling in their time with pleasurable activities once the drinking habit is broken. Occasionally, however, it may not be so straightforward and life may seem extremely empty and unrewarding without alcohol. A series of steps can be followed towards increasing pleasurable activities in your life.

Step 1

Learning to monitor pleasurable activities. An excellent first step is to get accurate information on your current levels of pleasurable activities by monitoring them (we already know of the benefits of self-monitoring from earlier exercises). You can do this quite easily by keeping a record of your activities during the week and rating how much pleasure you get from them. *Do not* include drinking as one of the pleasurable activities you are monitoring. This exercise is aimed at identifying all pleasurable activities other than drinking alcohol. The Activity Diary below is a typical record for logging activity patterns which will help you to structure your record keeping. When completing your diary, make sure that you state the activity you are engaged in and the levels of pleasure it gives you on a scale of 0–10. It is important you fill in your diaries regularly so you can monitor the changes in pleasure over the course of a 4–6 week period.

Activity Diary 2 is an example of a completed diary. Terry completed this diary at the beginning of his treatment. You may note that he was spending much of the week sleeping and getting little pleasure out of anything except being with his friends. It goes without saying that being with his friends also entailed much over-drinking.

Step 2

Developing a list of pleasurable activities. Once you have collected accurate information on what you are doing during the week, and what pleasure you obtain from your activities, you can begin listing pleasurable activities that you would like to initiate or increase in frequency that are not associated with drinking. Some of these pleasurable activities may well be things you used to take pleasure in but have not done for a long time. Others may be things you have wanted to do but never got round to trying.

William Glasser (a psychologist writing in the 1970s) argues that pleasurable activities can become 'positive addictions'. A negative addiction, such as alcohol, can be described as an activity that feels good at first but eventually results in feeling bad and causing harm. A positive addiction (e.g. swimming) is an activity that may not feel so good at first but usually becomes increasingly desirable and beneficial as time goes on.

An activity that is positively addictive meets the following criteria:

- It does not necessarily depend on others.
- It is non-competitive.
- It has some personal value.
- It can be improved with practice (but you are the only one who is aware of your progress).

Examples of pleasurable activities include exercise (swimming, cycling, jogging), hobbies, reading, practising

ACTIVITY DIARY: TERRY

Date: 5/5/09	Monday	Tuesday	Wednesday	Thursday	Friday	Saturday	Sunday
9–10	ASLEEP	ASLEEP	ASLEEP	ASLEEP	ASLEEP	ASLEEP	ASLEEP
10–11	ASLEEP	ASLEEP	ASLEEP	ASLEEP	ASLEEP	ASLEEP	ASLEEP
11–12	ASLEEP	ASLEEP	ASLEEP	ASLEEP	BREAKFAST P9	ASLEEP	ASLEEP
12–1	ASLEEP	ASLEEP	ASLEEP	ASLEEP	BREAKFAST P9	READ NEWSPAPER P9	ASLEEP
1–2	ASLEEP	ASLEEP	BREAKFAST P6	ASLEEP		WATCHED RACING P9	ASLEEP
2–3	ASLEEP	WATCHED NEWS P4	WATCHED TV P1	BREAKFAST P8		WATCHED RACING P9	ASLEEP
3–4	ASLEEP	WATCHED A FILM P6	WATCHED TV P1	CENTRAL LONDON P6		WATCHED RACING P9	ASLEEP
4–5	READ P7	SHOPPED P8	WATCHED TV P1	SHOPPED P7		WATCHED RACING P9	HANGOVER P0

5–6	READ P7	WATCHED TV P1	WATCHED TV P1	DINNER P3	OUT WITH FRIENDS P9	ASLEEP
6–7	READ P7	WATCHED TV P1	WATCHED TV P1	DINNER P3	OUT WITH FRIENDS P9	ASLEEP
7–12	TIDIED FLAT P5	WATCHED TV P1	MADE DINNER P9	WATCHED VIDEO P9	OUT WITH FRIENDS P9	DOZED P6

P = Pleasure (from 0 to 10)

ACTIVITY DIARY

Date:	Monday	Tuesday	Wednesday	Thursday	Friday	Saturday	Sunday
9–10							
10–11							
11–12							
12–1							
1–2							
2–3							
3–4							
4–5							
5–6							
6–7							
7–12							

P = Pleasure (from 0 to 10)

relaxation techniques (see Appendices 1 and 2 for tips on relaxation techniques and improving sleep), cultural pursuits and creative skills (art, writing, music). The following is an example of a list that was generated by a client:

Things I am doing but could do more of	Things I have never done but would like to do
Cinema	Acting workshops
Theatre	Pottery
Music gigs	Crossword puzzles
Walking and hiking	Jigsaw puzzles
Sport	
Snooker	
Wider reading	
Meet friends for a chat	
Listen to music	

Step 3

Developing a pleasurable activities schedule. Once you have a completed list of pleasurable activities you can start scheduling a small block of time each day (30–60 minutes) devoted to them. The goal is to *gradually* increase the activity levels and to maximize pleasure. You can begin this process by taking some time to sit quietly and mentally review your list of pleasurable activities. You will probably not want to do the same thing every day: perhaps exercise one day, work on a hobby another day and practising relaxation techniques on a third. Schedule some time each day, but do not schedule the activity, so that what you do in your personal time does not become an obligation. When you feel that you have achieved consistency, you can gradually increase to a more substantial block of time (1–2 hours). Remember to keep your activities in manageable proportions and define your personal success realistically.

Don't forget that putting a pleasurable activity schedule into action requires *commitment*. You must be prepared to establish priorities and possibly rearrange other activities in your life. The goal is to achieve an adequate *balance* between the activities you must do (eating, sleeping, working) and the activities you want to do (i.e. pleasurable ones). Schedule your pleasurable activities and make sure you can anticipate what problems or circumstances will interfere with your plans and how you will take care of them. Make sure you choose activities that you find *enjoyable*. Don't forget that some of the pleasurable activities you choose may initially not feel so good but will usually become increasingly desirable and beneficial as time goes on.

Step 4

Comparing activity diaries. Once you have a completed list of pleasurable activities, and have scheduled and engaged in pleasurable activities for a period of 4–6 weeks, return to your original Activity Diary and compare it with your current diary. Do you notice any differences? Before we analyze them let's take a quick look at Terry's example activity diary. Compare, for instance, the amount of sleeping in Activity Diary 2 and Activity Diary 3 (after 5 weeks of pleasurable activity scheduling). You will find that Terry gained an extra 24 hours of 'awake time' in the week (sleeping only 5 per cent of the day compared to almost 40 per cent before). His average pleasure ratings rose to an

ACTIVITY DIARY: TERRY

Date: 10/6/09	Monday	Tuesday	Wednesday	Thursday	Friday	Saturday	Sunday
9–10	WENT TO THE NEWSAGENT TO BUY A PAPER P4	WORKED ON COMPUTER P7	ASLEEP	ASLEEP	ASLEEP	ASLEEP	ASLEEP
10–11	BREAKFAST P8	WORKED ON COMPUTER P7	ASLEEP	ASLEEP	ASLEEP	WATCHED TV P6	ASLEEP
11–12	CALLED HELEN P8	WORKED ON COMPUTER P7	BREAKFAST P6	BREAKFAST P6	BREAKFAST P7	BREAKFAST P6	ASLEEP
12–1	WORKED ON COMPUTER P8	BREAKFAST P7	READ P6	NEWSPAPER P7	BREAKFAST P9	READ NEWSPAPER P5	BREAKFAST P7
1–2	LONG WALK P9	LONG WALK P6	WORKED ON COMPUTER P6	WATCHED RACING P7		SHOPPED P5	WORKED ON COMPUTER P7
2–3	LONG WALK P7	LONG WALK P6	WORKED ON COMPUTER P6	WATCHED RACING P7		WALK P5	WORKED ON COMPUTER P7
3–4	COFFEE P9	BANK P9	IT CLASS P6/7	WATCHED RACING P7	PHONED DOCTOR P6	WATCHED RACING P9	WORKED ON COMPUTER P7

ACTIVITY DIARY: TERRY (continued)

Date: 10/6/09	Monday	Tuesday	Wednesday	Thursday	Friday	Saturday	Sunday
4–5	AT HELEN'S P8	BOUGHT TICKETS BOUGHT FOOD FOR THIS EVENING P6	IT CLASS P6/7	ASLEEP	SHOPPED P6	WATCHED RACING P9	WORKED ON COMPUTER P7
5–6	AT HELEN'S P8	TALKED TO HELEN P9	SHOPPED P4	DINNER P6	WORKED ON COMPUTER P8	WATCHED RACING P9	READ P8
6–7	DINNER P8	WORKED ON COMPUTER P9	DINNER P6	WORKED ON COMPUTER P8	WORKED ON COMPUTER P8	DINNER P5	READ P8
7–12	CHATTED WITH HELEN P8	WORKED ON COMPUTER P9	TALKED TO JOE P8	WORKED ON COMPUTER P8	DINNER P3	WORKED ON COMPUTER P7	CHURCH P5

P 5 Pleasure (from 0 to 10)

average of 7/10 from 4/10, with all but one score at or above 5. The variety of pleasurable activities (not including drinking alcohol) increased and the exposure to drinking sprees with certain pals of his went down. Stopping to drink may have meant giving up a large chunk of recreation time and pleasure for Terry, but the presence of *alternative* pleasurable activities more than supplanted the loss.

Returning to comparing your diaries, estimate how much more *average* pleasure you get in a week from your current activities when compared with your original activities. You can calculate this by simply adding up all your pleasure scores and dividing them by the total number of scores. Do this for each week you have been monitoring your activities. Hopefully you will see that there is a trend towards increasing pleasure that goes hand in hand with an improvement in mood.

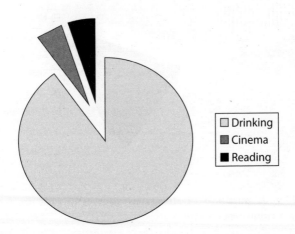

Figure 13.1 Sources of pleasure when drinking alcohol is a central activity

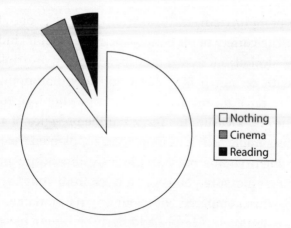

Figure 13.2 Sources of pleasure when drinking alcohol ceases

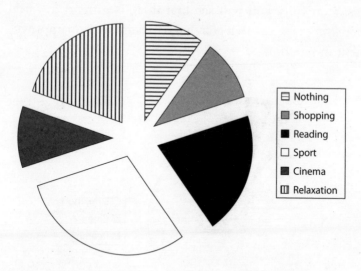

Figure 13.3 A 'portfolio' of alternative sources of pleasure when drinking alcohol has ceased

Scheduling pleasurable activities is one of the most powerful things you can do to improve your mood and at the same time inhibit your desire for drinking. If you have a problem with drinking, it is very likely that your main source of pleasure revolves around alcohol (see Figure 13.1).

However, if you stop drinking there would be much less left to give you pleasure (see Figure 13.2) This would increase the chances of slipping because you may be seeking pleasure but have few alternative ways of attaining it other than through drinking alcohol. That is why it is fundamental to build a *portfolio* of pleasurable activities (see Figure 13.3). This will ensure that there are other sources of pleasure in your life at your disposal, minimizing the need for alcohol use.

CHAPTER SUMMARY

- It is possible that when you stop drinking you might feel your life is empty.
- In order to counteract this feeling you need to build a series of pleasurable activities into your life.
- Over time you may become more conscious of the fact that you can substitute the short-term pleasures of alcohol with more long-term beneficial activities.

14

Building social support

Research evidence suggests that the involvement of a partner, friend and/or family members in dealing with problem drinking can, on the whole, bring positive results. For example, it has been shown that those who have established networks of supportive people tend to feel more confident about their ability to manage and cope with problems. A significant other can typically help by providing positive responses to stopping drinking, decreasing triggers for drinking, giving support for not drinking, and aiding access to further and new social support systems. Establishing a network of individuals that will provide support based on abstinence can also be very helpful. This reinforcement can be very straightforward, for example positive comments and encouragement or having a firm rule of 'no drink in the house'.

At times, however, significant others may engage in a number of behaviors that may increase cues for drinking. A husband who wants his wife to stop drinking may repeatedly nag her about the problems caused by drinking in the hope that his concerns will motivate change. Or a wife may try to get her husband to reduce his drinking by attempting to control his behavior through limiting access to alcohol or keeping a tight control over money. Such behaviors can frequently have unintended negative effects, causing tension, arguments and anger. This, in turn, is likely to lead to further drinking. Helpful family members and partners will need to learn to spot such behaviors and acknowledge the negative results arising from them. Learning alternative ways to discuss concerns about drinking may be helpful in aiding the problem drinker.

Partners, friends and family members can provide invaluable support by helping with the implementation of behavior changes and planning to avoid high-risk situations, discussing cravings and the general adoption of other cognitive and behavioral techniques and skills highlighted in this book.

For many problem drinkers important but difficult interactions with their children, partners and close friends may trigger drinking. Specific treatment for improving interpersonal relationships is another way for significant others to become involved in helping a person with problem drinking. These interventions may include transactional analysis therapy, couple or family therapy or parents skills training (see Useful Addresses section).

Some people have either no social support systems or ones that strongly support drinking. In such cases, it is important to gain access to new systems that can reinforce abstinence or that may prove incompatible with problem drinking. Self-help groups can be a source of such support; group activities such as walking, running, cycling or hiking can be another. Unfortunately, alcohol use can be an integral part of almost any activity. That is why it is important to look carefully at any activity group and establish whether the group norm includes drinking.

If you are a drinker, remember to go through the following steps when seeking new social support systems:

- Reflect on what kind of support you need. This may include help with problem-solving, resources, information or emergencies. This could range from information about flats for rent or small loans, to jobs, local clubs and community activities.
- Identify who might be of help. Friends with similar experiences, people who are important in your life and support your commitment to change and family members are some of the most commonly sought people for help.
- Think of how you can get the help you need. Strong relationships will take time and effort to build but some factors may be of particular help in this pursuit:
  - Actively listen. It is extremely important to pay attention to any advice that you are given. This will entail keeping appropriate eye contact, showing interest and sincerity, respecting personal space, not interrupting, asking questions for clarification and paraphrasing what has been said to ensure you have understood.
  - Provide feedback. People who you think will be of help will need your guidance about what is or

is not useful in their efforts to help you. Don't forget to thank them as this will maximize your chances of receiving more help in the future.

- Support others. A relationship where you help each other will be more reliable and satisfying than one in which the other person always gives but receives nothing. Helping someone out will not only benefit that person but will also strengthen your coping skills.

- Be specific. Whatever form of help you are looking for, be as specific and direct as possible in your request. This will increase the probability that you will get the help you need.

If you find it difficult to develop social support systems you may wish to consult a doctor, a CBT practitioner or an organization (see Useful Addresses section) that can offer extra support.

If you are a partner, family member or friend of someone with problem drinking you can help and support them by reading through this book, encouraging them to try the exercises and supporting them when the going gets tough. You will also find the information contained in Part One of this book helpful in increasing your understanding of this problem.

CHAPTER SUMMARY

- Involvement of significant others in dealing with problem drinking can bring, on the whole, positive results.
- A significant other can help by providing positive responses to drinking abstinence, decreasing cues for drinking, and giving support for not drinking, and aiding access to new social systems.
- If you have a drinking problem remember to go through the steps indicated when seeking new social support systems.
- If you are a partner, friend or family member of someone with a drinking problem, you can help and support them by reading through this book, encouraging them to try the exercises and supporting them when the going gets tough.

15

Moderating your drinking

Moderating your drinking (otherwise known as controlled drinking) is not easy, though it is a legitimate goal since some people can make a success of it. If you have used alcohol in an uncontrolled fashion over a long period of time, learning or relearning how to drink in a controlled way will entail applying basic skills that may not be that familiar to you. The most important skill of all for remaining within limits that you set for yourself is to slow down with your drinking. It takes some time for alcohol to bring its effects to bear and if you are drinking fast you may well be feeling the second drink while you are having your third or fourth. Consequently you may become convinced that it takes three or four drinks to get the effect you like when in reality it does not.

Another important reason for slowing down your drinking is to ensure you adjust your tolerance to alcohol. Tolerance (being able to hold your alcohol) is *not* a good thing. The more tolerant you are the larger doses of alcohol you will need to experience the same effect. Unfortunately, however, your body will still have to process it all. Alcohol tolerance

Table 15.1 Controlled drinking skills (Velleman, 1992)

Before drinking	While drinking
Eat something beforehand. Postpone going out. Don't drink in places where you have previously drunk heavily. Take little money. Take alcohol-free beverages with you.	Start off with a long soft drink. Drink half units. Dilute your alcoholic drinks. Drink in sips (time yourself). Alternate between non-alcoholic and alcoholic beverages. Avoid standing at the bar. Do not eat crisps and peanuts as they will make you thirsty. Practise drinking refusal skills. Distract yourself while drinking (e.g. play darts, have a chat). Try to go home early.

Table 15.2 Controlled drinking program (Velleman, 1992)

Key targets	What to remember	Strategic plan
Three days a week without a drink. No drinking before 7pm. No more than 3 units per day.	Alcohol-free days are Tuesday, Thursday and Sunday. Problem drinking is linked to wine, so all drinking will be limited to beer.	Eat something before you go out. Do not take more than £10 with you. Practise drinking refusal strategies. Always start with a non-alcoholic drink. Do something when you are there that does not only involve drinking.

adjusts in relation to what you drink. When you drink more, your tolerance will increase. As you cut back your drinking your tolerance decreases.

Some of the other tips you may find useful are outlined in Table 15.1.

Table 15.2 shows an example of a brief controlled drinking

program (for a typical week) that can serve as a template for building your own program:

Aim to drink well within the recommended limit set by the Department of Health, which is a maximum of 21 units per week for a healthy adult man and 14 for a healthy adult woman. As explained earlier, this threshold is measured in units. One unit is equivalent to:

- half a pint of ordinary-strength beer or lager
- one small glass of wine
- a single measure of spirits.

This translates into no more than 2–3 drinks per day. As part of your program you should also ensure that you do not drink every day. Three days a week without drinking is a reasonable target. Also, pick the controlled drinking skills from Table 15.2 that will work best for you.

Don't forget to continue self-monitoring what you actually drink. This is important for two reasons.

- It will give you a more tangible idea of what you are actually drinking.
- It will inform you if something is not going the way it should (i.e. you are drinking excessively).

You will need a contingency plan in case you fail to meet your controlled drinking program targets (i.e. you drink more than you have decided to). Ask yourself the following questions.

- Do I have someone to talk to if I end up drinking more than the allotted drinks per week?
- Do I have a partner, friend or family member to support a treatment goal of controlled drinking?
- Do I know the signs and symptoms of withdrawal and have access to an emergency phone number and hospital in the event that withdrawal symptoms occur?

If you *do not* have clear answers to all these questions, it may be wiser to stick to abstinence as a preferred goal. Remember that evidence shows that controlled drinking is more difficult than abstaining. The latter entails just avoiding drinking alcohol. Controlled drinking, however, is open to deliberate or accidental miscalculation on how much you may have drunk. In addition, you should not forget alcohol's disinhibitory properties which may cancel out your certainty of keeping to a prearranged limit once the first units have been drunk. Research suggests that people who are most successful at controlled drinking are those who are younger, employed, have a family around them, have only a short history of drinking problems, consume low levels before seeking help and show no signs of physical dependence.

CHAPTER SUMMARY

- Controlled drinking is not easy, though it is a legitimate goal since some people can make a success of it.
- Applying some basic skills and sticking to a controlled drinking program can help you achieve controlled drinking.
- Evidence shows that controlled drinking is more difficult than abstaining. Abstaining may thus be a better initial goal when tackling your drinking problem.

PART FOUR

Maintaining Change

16

Preventing slips

Sooner or later you may well find yourself in situations in which you are tempted to drink. You are probably very keen to ensure that if this happens you don't slip. This chapter is aimed at helping you build your confidence to deal with these situations if and when they occur.

If you have successfully managed to go through the book you may be experiencing a growing sense of control over your drinking. This feeling will usually continue until you encounter a high-risk situation. This is a situation in which an external or internal event poses a threat to your sense of control. Typical high-risk situations will include many of the activating events you have identified previously (e.g. negative emotions, social pressure, interpersonal conflict, a particular time of the day, certain places). There are several things you can do to tackle these high-risk situations: develop a personalized summary or blueprint of what you have learned from the program; keep clear in your mind how the problem drinking model works; develop a balanced lifestyle; and learn to identify and cope with warning signals that precede high-risk situations.

Building a personalized blueprint

Complete Exercise Sheet 14 to develop your individualized blueprint. Don't miss out any questions. An example of a completed blueprint follows.

EXERCISE 14: EXAMPLE BLUEPRINT

Understanding problem drinking
What is problem drinking and how does it develop?
Problem drinking involves drinking more than the recommended units of alcohol (either more than 21 units per week, or more than 4 units in single sessions), and/or drinking that causes problems with personal or work relationships.

What are the telltale signs of problem drinking?
Telltale signs of problem drinking include: drinking when you hadn't planned to; drinking more than you'd intended to; doing things after drinking that you wouldn't do sober; thinking you may well drink too much; thinking you need to change your drinking; trying but failing to modify drinking; regularly drinking alone; drinking in 'low-bottom' places; drinking often with heavy drinkers; drinking resulting in problems in personal/work relationships; others criticizing your drinking; thinking it is 'big' to be able to drink a lot.

Building motivation to change
How do you go about monitoring whether you have a problem with drinking?
A drinking diary can help with that. When do I drink? How much do I drink? Where do I drink? With whom do I drink? (I drank when feeling bad or bored. In a single session, I'd drink between 15 and 60 units of alcohol. I usually drank alone in pubs. When I did drink with others, it was usually with heavy drinkers. My drinking has caused me a long list of serious problems).

What are your concerns about change now and what were they before you started working through the program?

Before I started working through the program, I had various concerns about abstinence. 'My life might become boring and empty,' 'People might dislike or reject me,' 'I'll always be plagued by cravings.'

My life with alcohol was a nightmare. I have learned that drinking doesn't give me much pleasure and I felt I was in a 'black hole'. Not drinking has allowed me to incorporate a range of fun, pleasurable activities into my life and get satisfaction from and consistency in my work. I have an opportunity now to have a good career. No one has rejected me for not drinking. My family, colleagues and friends are pleased I'm not drinking. I won't lose anything of any value from not drinking. I am slightly concerned about cravings. I have managed cravings successfully many times in the past. I can do it again, especially as my motivation to stop drinking grows. Cravings will reduce in frequency and severity over time.

Implementing change

What different types of thought keep your drinking going?

Uncontrollability thoughts are general beliefs about your ability to control your drinking. These thoughts can work to make drinking episodes more likely or to sustain episodes. Uncontrollability thoughts arise from past drinking occurrences that provide evidence (or seem to provide evidence) for them. Such occurrences may involve drinking when you didn't intend to, drinking more than you intended to or drinking the morning after. Uncontrollability thoughts relevant to me are: 'I cannot control when I will start drinking,' 'Once I've started, I cannot stop,' or 'I'll drink the morning after.'

Permissive thoughts can work to sustain drinking once it has started. Permissive thoughts relevant to me are: 'I've started, so I might as well continue,' 'I can start afresh tomorrow,' 'Another few drinks and then I'll feel really good,' or 'I'll be up for coke if keep drinking.'

Positive thoughts can work to trigger drinking episodes. Positive thoughts relevant to me are: 'Drinking is the only way to rid myself of these unpleasant emotions,' 'Drinking will be exciting and make me feel good,' 'Drinking will relieve boredom,' or 'Drinking will result in my meeting a sexy woman and having sex with her.'

Uncontrollability thoughts – what is the evidence that you do have control over your drinking?

Consider the thought, 'I cannot control when I will start drinking.' Since I started CBT, I've had one slip. The vast majority of the time I have had control over the first drink. Since that slip, my motivation to stop drinking has increased. I realize that drinking makes the negative emotions worse, and the actual drinking isn't very enjoyable and I feel I'm in a 'black hole'.

Take the thought, 'Once I've started, I cannot stop.' It is not true that, once I've started drinking, I can't stop. I have drunk relatively moderately on some occasions during the last five years. However, drinking at all is a risky business. Past experience tells me that if I drink there's a good chance that I will drink to excess, especially if I start drinking quickly, I drink while upset or I desire cocaine while drinking.

Consider the thought, 'I'll drink the morning after.' There are many mornings after where I haven't drunk. I can make a choice the morning after not to drink and to start getting my life back on track, even if I feel rotten.

Permissive thoughts – what have you learned about these thoughts?

Consider the thought, 'I've started, so I might as well continue.' I have learned that the more I drink now, the worse I will feel for the next few days. Alcohol itself is a depressant; and past experience tells me that the more I drink the more likely I am to behave badly, which results in depression and anxiety.

Take the thought, 'I can start afresh tomorrow.' I have learned that the more I drink now, the worse I'll feel for the next few days and the harder it will be to resist drinking again. Also, a slip is a set-back. Although I won't be starting from square one, I will have suffered a set-back in my recovery.

Positive thoughts – what have you learned about these thoughts?
Take the thought, 'Drinking is the only way I'll get rid of these unpleasant emotions.' I have learned that any unpleasant emotions will disappear, naturally, over time; and I can do pleasurable activities to hasten their disappearance (e.g. running, country walks, cinema). Very importantly, I have learned that drinking makes my emotional state worse than it was before drinking. First, any troubling problems I had prior to drinking will still be there after drinking. Sometimes those same problems are made worse by drinking. Second, alcohol is a depressant and it depresses me for several days. Third, I almost always behave badly when I drink, which results in remorse, worsens depression and gives rise to anxiety.

Consider the thought, 'Drinking is exciting and will make me feel good.' My weekly activity monitoring sheet that I filled out during a slip, shows clearly that drinking brings very little pleasure, and is surrounded by a pleasure 'black hole' of feeling rough, depressed, and lethargic. Out of about twelve hours of actual drinking time, only three of those hours provided much pleasure (7 out of 10). I can get as much or more pleasure from other activities (e.g. reading novels, running, cinema, music, country walks) that have none of the costs or feelings of being in a 'black hole'. During the lapse, about six hours of actual drinking time were not at all enjoyable. I felt rough and bored. Don't get sucked into the gambler's fallacy, 'Next time, it will be really good.' That's not the reality.

Take the thought, 'Drinking will relieve boredom.' There are other non-destructive ways to relieve boredom (e.g. reading novels, music, exercise, film, phone friends). Boredom can be tolerated. Moods or problems, which are much worse than boredom (e.g. depression, anxiety, disruption), will follow drinking. As my weekly monitor shows, during my slip, I felt rough and bored for a significant amount of time while drinking. I may well get bored while drinking. Surrounding my drinking, during the slip, was a pleasure 'black hole'.

Take the thought, 'Drinking will result in meeting a sexy woman and having sex with her.' That virtually never happens when I drink. It's a pipedream. The reality of my drinking is that it isn't very pleasurable. I do things that I regret, I create problems for myself and I feel depressed and anxious after drinking. I am more likely to meet a sexy woman when sober, for instance, while on a country walk. I am better company and conversation when sober. Most women don't like guys who are pissed.

How can you tackle craving effectively? Is craving uncontrollable?
When I have a craving, I can consult my craving flashcard. It contains a coping statement, costs and benefits of drinking, distraction options, image replacement options and a delaying tactic.

Cravings are not uncontrollable. Cravings don't last forever. I have often resisted cravings, even severe ones. I can do it again. I know what to do. I have my improved flashcard. My motivation to stop drinking is high.

What are the benefits of increasing pleasurable activities?
Negative emotions or boredom can trigger positive thoughts. Positive thoughts can trigger cravings for alcohol. Cravings can increase the risk of drinking. By increasing pleasurable activities, I reduce the frequency or severity of negative emotions or boredom; as a result, I indirectly reduce the risk of drinking.

More generally, pleasurable activities teach me that I can lead a fun and interesting life without alcohol. They give me something to look forward to.

Pleasurable activities keep stress levels low and mood up. I can then tackle work in good spirits, and I have something in 'the bank' when difficult circumstances come up.

What effect does practising key skills have?

I have applied the problem-solving procedure to several decisions (e.g. decision to visit family, to go on holiday with family and to meet Francesca). This reduced my levels of concern. I generated and filtered more options than I would ordinarily have done. This led to my being happy with the decisions. I took into account any implications for drinking. I have also realized that I can apply the problem-solving procedure to emotional problems and to 'small' decisions relevant to drinking.

I learned a good refusal strategy. Rehearsing it increases the likelihood of my applying it. 'Would you like a drink? *I'll have a tomato juice, please.* Come on, have a real drink. I am not drinking at the moment. Why not? It doesn't agree with me. What do you mean? Can we talk about something else? Where are you going on holiday this year?'

What can be learned from apparently irrelevant decisions?

Apparently irrelevant decisions can work cumulatively to increase the risk of drinking. By reflecting on a previous slip, valuable information can be learned. Identify the situation in which the slip occurred and any decisions relevant to the slip. For each decision identified, identify alternatives. Assess the pros and cons of each alternative. Specify a safe alternative for each decision made that contributed to the slip.

In what ways can partners, family members and friends help with problem drinking?

Significant others can help with problem drinking by providing encouragement or praise for staying abstinent. This can increase motivation to stay abstinent. For instance, my father is very pleased that I have stopped drinking, and often comments that I am doing well with handling my problem drinking.

My father has provided a loan so that I can complete my training without taking on additional paid work. Additional paid work would have resulted in increased stress levels which would make abstinence difficult.

Doing things with friends or in a group provides a source of pleasure and socializing. It cuts out loneliness and improves mood, which is good for abstinence. I have joined a walking club, where drinking is of minor importance. I get positive feedback from others when on the walks and a lot of pleasure from the walking – good for abstinence and learning that a clean life can be a good, fun life.

EXERCISE 14
BLUEPRINT

Understanding problem drinking

What is problem drinking and how does it develop?

What are the telltale signs of problem drinking?

Building motivation to change

How do you go about monitoring whether you have problem with drinking?

What are your concerns about change now and what were they before you started working through the program?

Implementing change

What different types of thought keep your drinking going?

Uncontrollability thoughts – what is the evidence that you do have control over your drinking?

Permissive thoughts – what have you learned about these thoughts?

Positive thoughts – what have you learned about these thoughts?

How can you tackle craving effectively? Is craving uncontrollable?

What are the benefits of increasing pleasurable activities?

What effect does practising key skills have?

What can be learned from apparently irrelevant decisions?

In what ways can partners, family members and friends help with problem drinking?

Visualizing the problem drinking model

Another strategy that might help you when facing a high-risk situation is to visualize the problem drinking model (see Figure 16.1).

This will remind you of how 'mechanical' things can become when the vicious cycle gets going. It will also point to the variety of strategies that you can use to interrupt it at any stage. You can, for example, use the exercises highlighted in Chapter 15 to alter your thinking style, reducing the occurrence of negative emotions. Increasing pleasurable activities, exercising and relaxation techniques will also affect these directly. Identifying and challenging positive thoughts about drinking will help block the initiation of a drinking episode. In a similar fashion, identifying craving and its triggers, questioning its uncontrollability and using strategies to inhibit it will also serve to interrupt

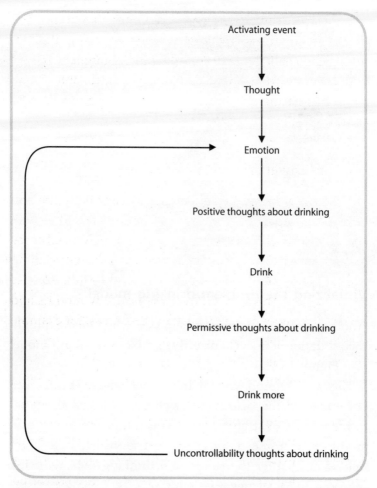

Figure 16.1 The problem drinking model

the link between positive thoughts about drinking and the initiation of alcohol use. Other skills that may come in handy involve developing drinking refusal techniques, learning to receive criticism about drinking and learning problem-solving. If a drinking episode does occur, identifying and challenging permissive thoughts will help to stop it. Identifying and challenging uncontrollability thoughts will give you crucial evidence that drinking is controllable. Don't forget that partners, family and friends can provide invaluable support in this process.

Working towards a balanced lifestyle

The degree of balance or imbalance in your daily life will have a big impact on the desire for indulgence in alcohol use. Ask yourself what areas of your life may need to be more balanced. These may include: interpersonal relationships, employment and finances, physical health, exercise and nutrition. Think ahead over the next few months and list the difficulties you may have in these areas, for example starting a new job, moving house, sorting out your finances or the birth of a baby. Write down ways in which these difficulties might be tackled. Make sure you draw on what you have learned from this program.

Whatever you decide to do to make your life more balanced, remember to do it in a gradual manner to avoid raising your expectations excessively. As you begin to change and feel better you may have surges of energy characterized by the need to make up for lost time. This may result in you taking on lots of responsibilities in one go: getting a new job, moving into a new home, retraining, engaging in major redecoration, cleaning out 20 years' worth of mess and so on. This enthusiasm for responsibility can be a double-edged sword: satisfying but also very tiring and unrewarding. At times, too much responsibility may end up leading you to question the value of not drinking. It is of paramount importance not to forget to schedule pleasurable activities in your life. Whatever you plan to do, ensure that you always identify an hour (or more) of the day when you can relax, read or exercise.

High-risk situations: what to do

The best way to avoid a slip is to learn to tackle high–risk situations effectively. Make a list of high-risk situations which could bring a resurgence of your problem. Once you have done this, write down what actions you would take to tackle them. This will probably involve going through your blueprint, the problem drinking vicious cycle, reviewing what you found helpful in the program and sticking to a balanced lifestyle. A sample plan to deal with warning signals can be found below:

HIGH-RISK SITUATIONS: WHAT TO DO

Upcoming social event: (1) assess risk (Where? When? Who?); (2) decide on whether to go; (3) rehearse drinking refusal exchange; (4) maintain motivation by reviewing blueprint and continuing with pleasurable activities; and (5) identify and take special precautions (e.g. prepare answers to thesis questions).

Social event: (1) remind myself that if I feel nervous, so will others; (2) utilize drinking refusal exchange; and (3) if I suffer from craving, go to toilet, read craving flashcard and decide whether to stay.

Old drinking pal: (1) avoid meeting where there's alcohol; and (2) only meet in safe circumstance (e.g. coffee at lunchtime).

Bored with work: (1) remind myself that everyone gets bored with work sometimes; (2) do some motivating work (e.g. search database or important reading); (3) schedule pleasurable activity (e.g. running or cinema); and (4) if I suffer from craving, review blueprint or use craving flashcard.

Stressed with work: (1) remind myself that work is hard for everyone; (2) review plans for future; (3) problem-solve if needed; (4) schedule pleasurable activity; and (5) if I suffer from craving, review blueprint or use craving flashcard.

Concerned with intellectual development: (1) schedule a time and date in which to think about development; and (2) if I suffer from craving, review blueprint or use craving flashcard.

Criticism: (1) remind myself that any anger or humiliation will go away over time; (2) do an absorbing, pleasurable activity (e.g. film, novel, music, exercise); and (3) if I suffer from craving, review blueprint or use craving flashcard.

Natural low: (1) remind myself that it is normal to feel low from time to time and it will pass; (2) get out of bed; (3) exercise; (4) schedule pleasurable activities; and (5) if I suffer from craving, review blueprint or use craving flashcard.

Doing little and bored: (1) remind myself a little boredom from time to time is normal and will pass; (2) sit with it or do something pleasurable; and (3) if I suffer from craving, review blueprint or use craving flashcard.

Alcohol desire: use craving flashcard.

PREVENTING SLIPS

Distraction: (a) describe surroundings; (b) phone friend but don't talk about desire; (c) do chores; (d) read a novel; or (e) play a video game.

Coping statements: 'Alcohol? No thanks. It leaves me feeling depressed, tired, rough, and anxious for at least a few days afterwards. It invariably leaves me feeling worse than I felt before drinking. No surprise there, for alcohol is a chemical depressant. It takes days for the body to recover; and drinking invariably exacerbates or creates problems (e.g. work problems, financial problems, health problems, emotional problems). Moreover, as my weekly log from my slip period shows, the actual drinking isn't much fun anymore, and I feel I'm in a "black hole". I behave badly when I drink, and then get stressed about it. I never pull. I can get at least as much pleasure, with none of the costs and no "black hole", from other activities (e.g. novels, cinema, music, meet friends or country walks).'

Images: Replace bad image with good image (e.g. standing strong, after run, on Parliament Hill, or giving a presentation).

Delay: Put off the decision whether to drink for 20 min.

Figure 16.2: An example of a slip prevention flashcard

Don't forget that if you have learned and can implement effective coping responses to deal with high-risk situations the probability of a slip will decrease significantly.

Developing a flashcard

You can sum up all the information on preventing slips on a flashcard. This will be of invaluable use when a warning signal occurs and you need to tackle it quickly and effectively. An example of completed flashcard is shown in Figure 16.2.

CHAPTER SUMMARY

- Sooner or later you may well find yourself in situations in which you are tempted to drink.
- You can tackle these by:
  - Developing a blueprint of what you have learned.
  - Reminding yourself of the problem drinking model.
  - Working towards a balanced lifestyle.
  - Identifying high-risk situations and warning signals, and planning to deal with them.
  - Developing a flashcard.

17

What to do if a slip does occur

Since change is a cyclical process it is unlikely that you will be completely successful on your first attempt to alter your drinking behavior. You are probably already aware of this and may have well gone through the stages of change several times. If a slip does occur you have to remind yourself that progress towards your goal will never be linear as you would want it to be (as in Figure 17.1) but rather a bit of a bumpy ride (as in Figure 17.2).

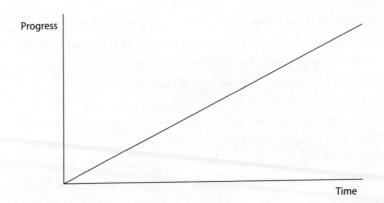

Figure 17.1 Unrealistic idea of progress: linearity

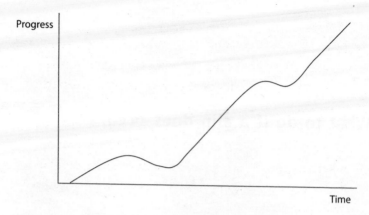

Figure 17.2 Realistic idea of progress: a 'bumpy' ride

If a slip occurs, you have to ensure that you immediately put it in context:

• It is not a catastrophe

Rather, it is an integral part of what you are trying to do: *practice 'unlearning' old drinking behaviors* and replacing them with *new behaviors*. As with everything that needs practice it won't be easy, and there will be times when you will have to pick yourself up and start all over again. What you will probably find by persisting is that things get easier and that even if you do slip a few times you won't think it is the end of the world and you will get over it quickly.

The following strategies for coping with slips may be of help:

- *Stop what you are doing.* If a slip occurs, stop what you are doing and observe what is happening. The slip is a consequence of not having properly acknowledged a high-risk situation.

- *Don't panic.* The instinctive reaction to a slip may be to blame yourself and feel extremely guilty about what's happened. This reaction is normal. Remember that every negative emotion will eventually subside, including this one!

- *Remember what you have done to date.* Go back to your summary of the work you have done during the program. Think back over the reasons that made you decide to change your drinking behavior. Renew your commitment to change.

- *Analyze the situation that brought about the slip.* Rather than blame yourself or someone else, find out what happened. It was probably a unique event. Try to identify what led up to it and what warning signals preceded it.

- *Kick-start the recovery.* Get back in action by reviewing what you have accomplished to date and start again with the key strategies you know will work: remove yourself from high-risk situations and engage in pleasurable activities.

- *Seek help.* Ask partner, friends or family to help you in any way they can. If you are alone seek out the assistance of professionals or self-help groups.

CHAPTER SUMMARY

- Since change is a cyclical process it is unlikely that you will be completely successful on your first attempt to alter your drinking behavior.
- If a slip does occur, remind yourself that progress towards your goal will probably never be linear but will have ups and downs that get smoother over time.
- If a slip does occur:
  - Don't panic.
  - Stop what you are doing.
  - Remember what you have done to date.
  - Analyze the situation that brought the slip.
  - Kick-start the recovery.
  - Develop a blueprint of what you have learned from the slip.
  - If you feel particularly helpless seek assistance from partner, friends, family, professionals or self-help groups.

18

Problem drinking and negative emotions: A closer look

If we were able to get rid of both anxiety and depression, the bulk of our negative emotions would be gone. As a result there would be few problems with excessive alcohol use. Unfortunately we cannot rid ourselves entirely of either anxiety or depression. What we can do is learn to cope with these negative emotions in a constructive and effective way – a way that does NOT entail using excessive amounts of alcohol.

Anxiety

Research shows that a high percentage of people experiencing problems with alcohol also experience problems with anxiety, a negative mood usually characterized by bodily symptoms of physical tension and apprehension about the future. Depending on the situation, you might also call this experience 'fear' or 'worry'. Ultimately, however, these are just labels for something that feels bad and uncontrollable, and is unwanted. There is one important point to note, however:

- Anxiety does not last forever

It affects us all, to different degrees, but we are simply not 'wired up' to go on experiencing it *ad infinitum*. Eventually our brain will adjust our system and our anxiety levels will *naturally* subside. This process is called *habituation*. Whether it's a spider phobia, fear of experiencing a panic attack away from home or a powerful concern that people will think us inadequate, if we stay long enough with the anxiety (i.e. we do not try to control it or escape from it) it will start subsiding. You may believe and feel that anxiety will last forever, but in reality it will not, habituation will eventually kick in (see Figures 18.1 and 18.2).

In addition, the more we expose ourselves to what makes us anxious, the easier it will become to tolerate the anxiety (see Figure 18.3).

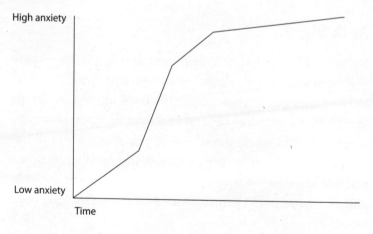

Figure 18.1 Anxiety: how it may feel – like it's lasting forever

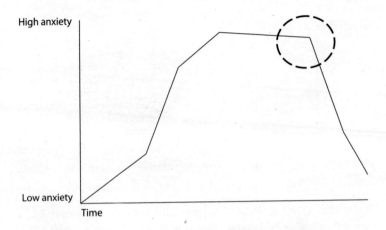

Figure 18.2 Anxiety: how it actually behaves – it will eventually come down

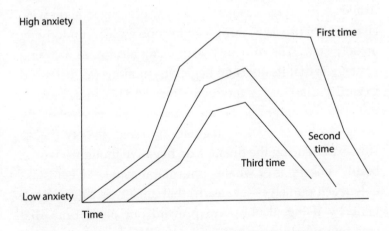

Figure 18.3 Anxiety: repeated exposure will make it increasingly tolerable

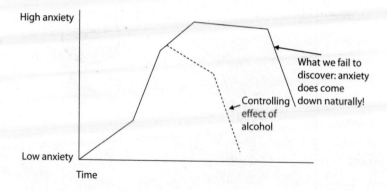

Figure 18.4 Effect of alcohol: temporarily reduces the anxiety but does not allow us to discover that it will come down naturally

Many of those who suffer from problem drinking had a history of anxiety problems *before* they became problem drinkers. It is thus reasonable to view prolonged and excessive alcohol use as a learnt way to cope with an underlying anxiety state. The difficulty with using alcohol as a coping strategy is that its effect on negative emotions (as discussed in earlier chapters) is very temporary and becomes increasingly so the more one becomes dependent on alcohol. By using alcohol to control, regulate or avoid anxiety (i.e. to stop experiencing the dread, fear, negative thoughts, worry, bodily sensations or whatever form it may take) we mistakenly teach ourselves (i.e. learn) that anxiety is *only* controllable by using alcohol. We prevent ourselves from discovering whether anxiety will actually come down naturally (see Figure 18.4). See also Helen Kennerley's *Overcoming Anxiety* (details in the References and Further Reading section) for more help.

In addition, alcohol actually worsens our anxiety and offers no real solutions to it. This makes it harder to stop drinking because if we do we will have to face more and 'new' anxiety (see Figure 18.5).

What happens next? We may increase our alcohol use in order to cope with growing and 'new' anxiety (= original anxiety + anxiety induced by alcohol use). This will, in turn, bring about a 'third generation' anxiety, which will be dealt with by more alcohol use, and so on. Figure 18.6 shows how the upward spiral of anxiety and problem drinking *takes off*.

Causes of anxiety

Anxiety has no simple one-dimensional cause, but comes from multiple sources.

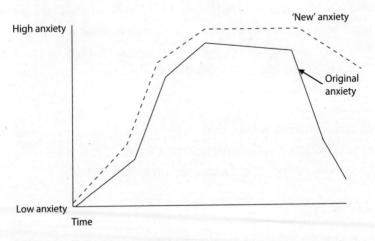

Figure 18.5 Effect of alcohol: makes the anxiety worse over time

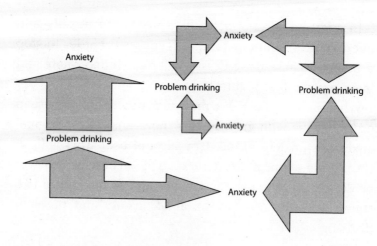

Figure 18.6 Simple model of the effect of problem drinking on anxiety

Biology and family history

We are all hard-wired to experience certain anxieties, fears and worries, for example fear of spiders, snakes, water, thunder, heights, separation and strangers. This is a necessary evolutionary development because it protects us from dangers in the environment. It also suggests that fears can be encoded in our genes and as such there is the possibility that they can be passed on in families. In partial support of this, evidence shows that anxiety problems run in families, although it is difficult to know whether this is because of genetic or learning factors or a mixture of both.

Life stresses

Life stresses come in two basic forms: a distinct stressful event, such as a sudden tax demand, being made redundant or a road accident; or a continuous process, such as chronic financial problems, a long-term physical illness or an exceedingly demanding job. Research evidence shows that stressful events have been linked with the onset of emotional and psychological problems. In particular 'threat events' (such as the ones mentioned above) have been linked with the onset of anxiety-related problems.

Thinking style

Thinking biases, such as catastrophizing, generalizing, jumping to conclusions with little evidence, ignoring positives and only focusing on negatives, all contribute to the development and maintenance of anxiety problems. Thinking biases tend to be learned at an early stage in life, usually by modelling parents' own thinking styles. But as with everything that is learned, we can 'unlearn' to think in negative and biased ways.

Coping strategies

The majority of the population has good coping strategies for managing anxiety problems and most of us develop, over time, good ways of coping without help. The universal coping strategies involve trying to keep busy, doing exercise, spending time with friends and other forms of distraction. We may also actively face that which makes us anxious and attempt to problem-solve. Unfortunately we all sometimes use unhelpful coping strategies that run the risk of making the problem worse. These typically include more readily available coping strategies such as comfort eating or drinking, completely avoiding any trigger of what makes us anxious or spending too much time focusing on the anxiety and worrying about it!

Social support

Our vulnerability to anxiety increases with reduced levels of social support. Social support can take many forms, from a single person to confide in, to a wide network of friends or workmates. The greater the social support, the more protected we are against trauma and ongoing stresses. Social support is thus particularly important at those times of major life crises.

Vulnerability to anxiety-related problems is thus determined by a constellation of factors. Nobody escapes anxiety since, to a large extent, it is there to help us survive. Anxiety only becomes a problem when it is exaggerated and when a cycle of distress develops. We can learn to break this cycle and deal with our anxiety by understanding how our problem arose in the first place (by examining personal and social risk factors such us our family history, social support and stressful events) and how it is maintained (by identifying what thinking style, coping strategies and stresses may be present today).

Depression

Most of us know what it is like to feel depressed: we have all experienced negative states in which we repeatedly think about negative themes, feel the need for reassurance, brood about unpleasant events and feel pessimistic about the future. We may feel hopeless, guilty, unmotivated and completely uninterested in what usually are pleasurable activities. But there is an important point to note:

> • For 99 per cent of people these states do not last forever.

Though to some degree it affects us all, chances are that we are not going to go on experiencing a depressive episode for the rest of our lives, though it may feel this way when we are in the midst of one (see Figure 18.7).

Eventually we come out of a depressive episode and there are plenty of things we can do to ensure that this happens sooner rather than later (such as scheduling pleasurable activities and challenging our ways of thinking).

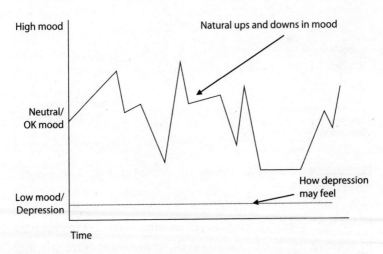

Figure 18.7 The natural ups and downs of our moods compared with how depression may feel

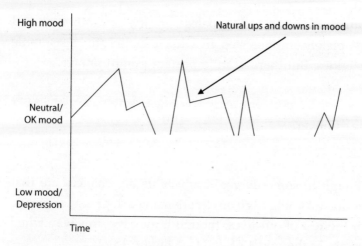

Figure 18.8 Short-term effects of alcohol use on low mood/depression: the 'erasing' effect

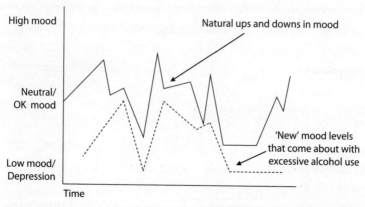

Figure 18.9 Long-term effects of alcohol use on low mood/depression

Drinking excessive amounts of alcohol is *NOT* a useful way to achieve this goal, even though, in the short-term, alcohol can make us feel as though we have *erased* any low mood

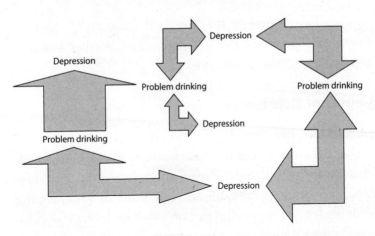

Figure 18.10 Simple model of the effects of problem drinking on depression

(see Figure 18.8). In the long-term, however, once the effect of alcohol fades away we are worse off (see Figure 18.9).

It is thus reasonable to view prolonged and excessive alcohol use (as with anxiety) as a learnt behavior to cope with depression. The problem with this coping strategy is that it is only very short term and becomes increasingly so the more we grow to be dependent on alcohol. Don't forget that alcohol is a toxin and that large amounts of it *produce* depression; conversely, when we stop using it, depression will often subside.

By using alcohol to control, regulate or avoid depression we are again mistakenly teaching ourselves that depression is *only* controllable by using alcohol. We prevent ourselves from discovering whether we could find alternative ways of coming out from a low mood, thus engendering an upward spiral of depression and problem drinking that looks all too familiar (see Figure 18.10). See Paul Gilbert's *Overcoming Depression* (details in the References and Further Reading section) for further assistance.

Causes of depression

Depression, like anxiety, has no simple one-dimensional cause, but comes from multiple sources. These share many characteristics with the common causes of anxiety, including biology/ family history, life stresses, thinking style, coping style and social support. A person's vulnerability to depression is thus determined by a variety of factors rather than by any single element. Depression only becomes a problem when it is exaggerated and when a cycle of distress develops. We can learn to break this cycle and deal with our depression by understanding how it arose (by examining personal and social risk factors such us our family history, social support and stressful events) and how it is maintained (by identifying what thinking style, coping strategies and ongoing stresses may be present today).

Some of the behavioral strategies that you may have already implemented (such as scheduling pleasurable activities, exercising, using relaxation techniques, reducing your alcohol intake) will have brought a significant improvement in mood and/or reduction in anxiety.

CHAPTER SUMMARY

- If excessive drinking is a problem you are experiencing, it is very likely that this is due in large part to negative emotions that have not been properly resolved.

- Negative emotions like anxiety and depression are not designed to last forever: they decrease over time.
- If you engage in problem drinking, anxiety and depression will be magnified.
- Prolonged and excessive alcohol use is a learnt behavior to cope with negative emotions. But it is very short term and becomes increasingly so the more you become dependent on alcohol.
- If alcohol use has featured in your life as a coping strategy for a long period of time, you may not be entirely conscious of the above processes.
- Dealing with negative emotions will help in gaining control over your drinking.

19

Tackling negative emotions:
Thinking differently, feeling differently

As discussed in Chapter 18, negative emotions, such as anxiety, depression, worry and anger can trigger problem drinking. (See Appendices 3 and 4 for advice on dealing with worry and anger.) In order to successfully tackle any drinking problem these negative emotions will have to be addressed. Frequently, these emotions result from assuming a negative thinking style about events that could straight-forwardly be interpreted as positive or neutral. We thus tend to assume situations or events make us feel bad, when, in most cases, our thoughts about these events determine how we feel. The chain linking events, thoughts, emotions and behaviors can be summarized as in Figure 19.1.

Can you think of an example, from your own life, that illustrates this chain of events? You may find it hard. Most people will argue in favour of the model in Figure 19.2.

Thoughts frequently 'bridge' activating events and nega-tive emotions. Usually changing your thinking will make you feel better, though this will not happen overnight. It will take time and practice before you learn to spot your-self thinking negatively and adopt a more positive thinking

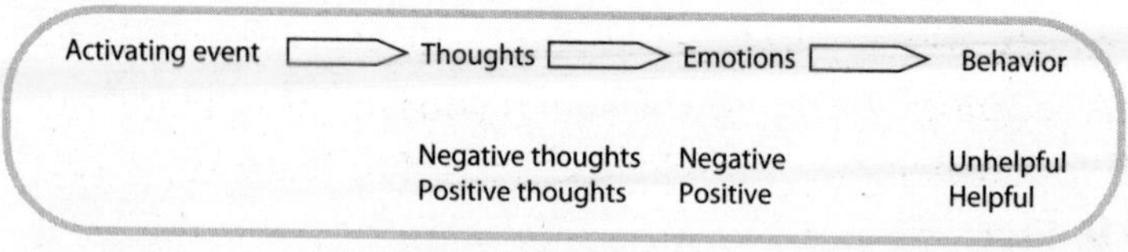

Figure 19.1 Chain linking events, thoughts, emotions and behaviors

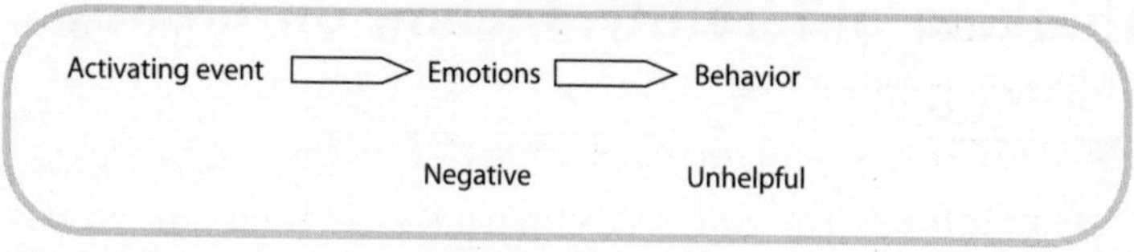

Figure 19.2 Chain linking events, emotions and behaviors

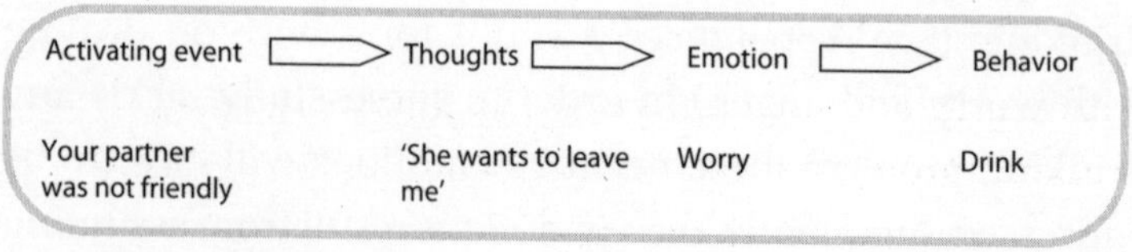

Figure 19.3 Negative emotion chain

style. See Figure 19.3 for an example of a negative emotion chain.

There are several things you can do to change your thoughts. The first step is to learn to *spot yourself thinking*

Activating event	Thoughts	Emotions
A work colleague was unfriendly	....	Tension
	....	
	....	
Somebody says you are no good	....	Depression
	....	Anxiety
	....	

negatively. What kinds of negative thinking habit have become automatic for you? Usually your negative emotions will follow negative thinking patterns. For instance, if you are feeling anxious there is a good chance you were thinking negatively just before that.

Can you think of thoughts that might be linked to some negative emotion or activating event? You can begin with the following examples:

Ellis (1975) has put forward types of thought that may not be helpful. Can you recognize any of them in your range of thoughts?

- Self-put downs. 'I am pathetic'; 'I am worthless.'
- Expecting the worst. 'It will never work'; 'All my relationships are doomed.'
- Unrealistic goals. 'I must do everything right'; 'Other people should always be reliable.'
- Catastrophizing. 'If things do not go my way it will be the end of the world.'
- Black and white. 'If I am not completely loved all the time it must mean I am loathed.'
- Overgeneralization. 'I am always going to be nervous'; 'I will never be on time.'

Stopping these thoughts and *replacing them* with more neutral and constructive thoughts will help you to feel less depressed, anxious, angry, upset or tense. In other words you will start feeling better about yourself. For example, if a work colleague calls you a 'waste of space' you can:

- Let that depress you, which will mean that you are thinking something on the lines of, 'Yes, he is right, I am no good.'

or . . .

- Let that anger you which will mean that you are thinking something on the lines of, 'How dare he say this about me?'

or . . .

- You can challenge the negative thinking with more positive thoughts, such as, 'Perhaps he has had a row with his partner and is taking it out on me. I know my worth. If I did do something wrong, I will put it right.'

These last thoughts may literally *produce* a better mood.

You should always ask yourself whether there are different ways to interpret situations, events, people's comments and so on. You should also try to replace negative thoughts (which can be automatic to an extent) with more positive ones. The following are some strategies that can help 'neutralize' negative thinking patterns:

- *Decatastrophizing*. Many times negative emotions arise from predicting catastrophic consequences. These thoughts can be challenged by examining the probability of feared events actually happening and your ability to prevent them from occurring.
- *Recalling positive things about yourself*. Remind yourself of things that you usually do well. For example what nice things have others said about you or done for you? What is good about you as a person?
- *Challenging extreme thinking*. Thoughts that have 'shoulds', 'musts' and 'oughts' signal extreme thinking. Contrast: 'My partner should love me for everything I do' with 'It is nice if my partner wholeheartedly loves me, but he [she] does not have to like everything I do'.
- *Mindfulness*. Try and become aware of your thoughts and how they are linked to your negative emotions. Learn to recognize that anxiety, depression and anger are all signals that your thoughts and actions may need constructive change.
- *Self-reward*. If you manage to handle a difficult situation well, reward yourself. For example: 'I began by being upset that I was not invited to a friend's party, but I did a good job at recalling positive things about myself and challenging my extreme thinking'.

We have discussed basic techniques for managing thoughts associated with negative emotions that often precipitate drinking episodes. If you feel that you need specific help for negative emotions you are experiencing, you may find it useful to consult other books from the Overcoming series (see References and Further Reading section) that deal with specific issues (e.g. depression, anxiety, worry) or get in touch with your doctor.

CHAPTER SUMMARY

- Negative emotions can frequently result from assuming a negative thinking style about events that could simply be interpreted as positive or neutral.
- The first step towards changing your negative thoughts involves spotting yourself thinking negatively.
- The second step towards changing your negative thoughts involves stopping and replacing negative thoughts.
- If you feel that you need more specific help for negative emotions you may be experiencing, consult other books from the Overcoming series (see References and Further Reading section) that deal with negative emotions or get in touch with your doctor.

20

A final word

The methods described in this book are intended to help you break the problem drinking vicious cycle. On first impression they may appear straightforward and almost simplistic. The reality is that implementing them success-fully will take time and effort. In order to make the most of your efforts for change, as well as to keep track of progress, you should have easy access to all your exercise sheets and take time to review them regularly. If you do not do this and experience a slip, you may well be tempted to think that your improvement was illusory and temporary.

You may be wondering whether it matters which of the strategies for overcoming problem drinking you start with. The strategies presented in this book follow a specific order because treatment would typically progress on these lines. But the order is not invariable and you may find that starting with different strategies can also benefit you. When you have decided which of the strategies to start with, ensure that you give it a fair try before you move to something else. It can be tempting to change a strategy if it does not appear to be helpful at first. Stick to each one until you feel sure you understand how it works and try to be realistic about what you want to do. It is better to stick to small targets and be successful than to try to do everything in one go and feel you have failed. Don't forget that success breeds success: it does not matter how small the initial success is. Make sure that when you have had one successful experience you do not just leave things there, but you try the same thing again. In this way you will be able to consolidate your gains. Tackle bigger and harder targets once you have built your confidence and know more about how the strategies work for you.

Appendix 1:

Relaxation

Anxiety and stress can cause muscular tension which in turn gives rise to a range of unpleasant physical sensations that can act as a trigger for drinking. These sensations can be controlled by learning and practising a series of relaxation exercises. Over time you should become proficient at responding to physical tension by using these exercises which in turn will promote mental tranquillity and reduce the risk of drinking. Some of these exercises are outlined below.

Controlled breathing

Breathing is an automatic bodily activity that is performed without much conscious awareness. At times of physical exertion and stress we tend to breathe rapidly and in a shallow way. This rapid breathing has a function: we take more oxygen into our bloodstream which makes it easier for us to sustain physical exertion (such as running away from danger). It is a normal response to demanding situations and when performed over short periods of time it is not a problem.

Rapid breathing, also known as overbreathing or hyper-ventilation, can become a problem when it lasts for long periods of time. This is because rapid breathing causes too much oxygen to enter our bloodstream, leading to numerous unpleasant bodily sensations: dizziness, visual problems, exhaustion and chest and stomach pains. All these can be quite frightening and can lead to escalations in anxiety and more rapid breathing which in turn can result, occasionally, in a full-blown panic attack.

Controlled breathing is a technique that can help you normalize your breathing pattern at times of stress and anxiety. Breathing exercises have been found to be effective in reducing panic attacks, depression, irritability, muscle tension, headache and fatigue.

Common misconceptions

'It is boring to practice something I do automatically'. That can be the case. But if symptoms of stress and anxiety are your problem, you may want to give this technique a try. This is a very efficient way of reducing the muscle tension present with stress and anxiety-related symptoms or thoughts.

How do you do it?

1 *Sit or lay down*. If you are sitting make sure your back is straight. Place your palms on your belly. Place the tip of your tongue against the roof of your mouth and keep it there throughout the exercise.
2 *Inhale slowly* (to a mental count of four) and quietly through your nose. Let the breath travel through to

your belly. You will notice your belly rising underneath your palms.

3 *Hold your breath*. Hold it for a mental count of five.

4 *Exhale slowly through your mouth*. Exhale completely
through your mouth, making a whoosh sound to a
count of eight. Pause.

5 *Repeat steps 2–4*. Take eight to twelve of these relaxing
breaths and let yourself experience the feeling of
relaxation.

Are you doing it right?

It can be difficult to inhale deeply into your abdomen especially if you have been very tense and have been shallow
breathing habitually. It may help if you make your exha-
lation as long as possible. Pause for a mental count of five
and then inhale again. Repeat several times. The in-breath
will deepen and you will feel it in your abdomen.

How often should you do it?

Repeat whenever you feel the need to do it.

Progressive muscular relaxation (PMR)

PMR was developed by Chicago doctor, Edmund Jacobsen,
in the 1930s. The PMR program involves alternately tensing
and relaxing different muscle groups, which leads to deep
relaxation. This technique is based on the premise that the
body responds to stressful events and thoughts with muscle
tension. This bodily tension increases the subjective expe-

rience of anxiety and stress. So with deep muscular relaxation the bodily tension is reduced, in turn leading to a decrease in subjective feelings of anxiety and stress.

Scientific research has shown that PMR is beneficial in the treatment of muscular tension, anxiety, insomnia, depression, irritable bowel syndrome, fatigue, muscle spasms, high blood pressure, neck and back pain, mild phobias, stress and stuttering. Running through a PMR session takes around 15 minutes.

Common misconceptions

'I don't have time and I cannot relax easily.' Think whether it is worth giving it a try. After all, it takes only 15 minutes and the benefits can be enormous. Don't forget that practice makes perfect. Do not give up before you've even tried. Give it a go and be patient with yourself. It can take one or two weeks to master the technique.

How do you do it?

1 *Find a quiet place.* It may help if you turn out the lights or draw the curtains. Try to minimize the noise. The fewer distractions you have, the easier it will be to concentrate. A moderate room temperature and comfortable clothing may help as well. It is better if you are neither full nor hungry when you begin.

2 *Make yourself comfortable.* Sit or lie down comfortably, close your eyes and take a few deep breaths.

3 *Practice the basic movement: tense and relax.* Starting

with your feet, tense your muscles by pulling the toes upwards. Do not strain, and concentrate on the sensation of tension. Hold for about 5 seconds, release quickly and then relax for 10 to 15 seconds. Observe how your muscles feel when you relax them. Repeat.

4 *Progress in turn with different parts of the body.* If there is a particular place where you feel more tension, repeat the basic movement for longer:

- *Legs* – straighten your legs, point your toes upwards, tense and hold for 5 seconds. Relax, let your legs go limp. Repeat.
- *Buttocks and thighs* – squeeze, hold for 5 seconds and release. Repeat.
- *Abdomen* – squeeze your abdominal muscles tightly against your spine. Hold and then release. Repeat.
- *Back* – arch your back. Feel the tension and hold. Release and repeat.
- *Arms* – stretch out your arms and hands. Clench your fists and hold. Release, let your arms and hands go limp. Repeat.
- *Shoulders and neck* – lift your shoulders up and draw them as close as you can. Press your head back. Release and repeat.
- *Face* – tense your forehead and jaw. Close your eyes and squeeze. Bite hard. Release. Drop your jaw and slightly open your mouth. Repeat.
- *Whole body* – tense your entire body. Hold the tension for a few seconds and then release rapidly. Repeat a few times.

5 *Focus on your breath.* When you have finished the practice, take a few deep breaths. Place your hands on your belly and observe the rhythmical movement. Spend a few minutes doing so. Get up slowly and move gently.

Are you doing it right?

It may take a while to get the hang of it. The benefits come with practice. If it feels good, you are probably doing it right. You could make your own recording, reading the relaxation script. Just make sure you read it slowly!

How often should you do it?

You may want to start with an evening session first to help you unwind after work and then build in a morning session as well. After you've mastered the technique you can practice a shorter version, which might involve tensing and relaxing your entire body or just those places that feel particularly tense. Or simply omit the 'tense' stage and relax different muscle groups in the sequence.

Brief relaxation

The Brief Relaxation Procedure (BRP) was developed by cardiologist Herbert Benson. He wanted to help cardiac patients reduce the stress which worsened their condition. This simple but very effective relaxation procedure has since become established for reducing the symptoms of stress and stress-related illnesses.

As its name suggests, BRP is brief and can be practised anywhere: during your lunch or tea break, while stuck in a traffic jam, on the tube or bus – the opportunities are plentiful. A variant of this relaxation procedure is given below.

Common misconceptions

'I can't switch off easily.' Practice makes perfect. Don't give up before you've even tried. Give it a go and be patient with yourself. It can take a while before you master the technique and truly benefit from the practice.

How do you do it?

1 *Think of an image which you find calming.* The image could be of a beach on a sunny summer day, or a garden, a view from a mountain. In fact, it could be anything personally relevant or meaningful to you which brings sensations of calmness.

2 *Sit comfortably.* It may help if you turn out the lights and draw the curtains. Try to minimize the noise. The fewer distractions you have, the easier it will be to concentrate.

3 *Close your eyes.* Imagine your body growing heavier and heavier. Feel the warmth from within your body and let yourself feel relaxed.

4 *Breathe slowly.* Breathe through your nose, and as you exhale think of the chosen image. Hold the image in your mind. Breathe regularly.

5 *Keep going for as long as it takes you to feel relaxed.*

Your mind may wander off to the events of the day, or a worry that you have. Do not dwell on them. Do not try not thinking of them. Just accept them as thoughts and draw your attention back to your chosen image and to your breathing.

Are you doing it right?

If it feels good, you probably are doing it right.

How often should you do it?

Whenever you feel tense.

Meditation

Scientific studies have shown various benefits of regular meditation: boosting of the immune system, which enables the body to better fight off disease, numerous changes in the brain functioning, leading to a decrease in stress responses, and increased contentment and happiness. More and more doctors recommend meditation to reduce the negative effects of stress and anxiety. It has also been used as an add-on treatment for depression, hyperactivity and attention deficit disorder. Meditation may prevent or at least aid control of the pain of chronic problems like cancer, heart conditions and AIDS. You don't need to become a Buddhist monk or a Yogi to reap the benefits. Even a 10-minute daily session can bring about dramatic effects.

Common misconceptions

'It isn't for me. You've got to be a Buddhist or a hippy to practice meditation.' If these kinds of thought are going through your head you are mistaken. More and more people are taking up regular meditation, from celebrities such as Sting, Shania Twain, Goldie Hawn and Richard Gere to politicians such as Al Gore and business people such as Bill Ford (head of Ford Motors)

How do you do it?

There are hundreds of meditation techniques. You may want to search for the one that will feel right for you. Here is an example of a quick meditation that you can adopt to start with.

1 *Find a quiet place.* It may help if you turn out the lights and draw the curtains. Try to minimize the noise. The fewer distractions you have, the easier it will be to concentrate. A moderate room temperature and comfortable clothing may help as well. It is better if you are neither hungry nor full when you begin.
2 *Sit comfortably.* Sit on a chair or on the floor or wherever you are comfortable. Rest your hands in your lap. Keep your back straight without tightness, and the chin pulled in a little.
3 *Close your eyes.* By closing your eyes you will be able to shut out the external world.
4 *Focus on your breath, a word or phrase.* Concentrate

on your breathing, on the inhaling and exhaling and the rhythmical movement of your chest. Breathe slowly and regularly. Spend a few minutes doing so. Find a word or a simple phrase that means something to you, that has a soothing effect. If nothing comes to your mind say 'om', or 'calm' or 'love'. Try saying your word or phrase to yourself with every out breath. Say it again and again.

5 *Accept intrusions*. You will notice that your mind will wander off to the events of the day, or a worry that you have. Some thoughts may pop up in your head out of the blue. Do not worry or dwell on them. Do not try not thinking of them. Just accept them as thoughts and draw your attention back to your word/phrase and to your breathing. Continue meditative practice for 10 minutes, or as long as you feel that you need to.

Are you doing it right?

It may take a while to get the hang of it. The benefits come with practice. If it feels good, you probably are doing it right.

How often should you do it?

As often as you can or if it feels good. You may want to start with an evening session first to help you unwind after work and then build in a morning session as well. Make this your 'meditation time'.

Yoga

There are many different types of yoga styles. Here are the main characteristics of some of them:

- Hatha yoga – gentle and soothing.
- Ashtanga (or Astanga) – vigorous, power yoga that will make you sweat.
- Ananda – gentle style that prepares you for meditation.
- Bikram – stretching and warming.
- Sivananda – stretching and meditative.

Yoga is a powerful, non-competitive and invigorating physical activity. Some of the physical benefits of yoga include: better flexibility, balance and coordination, toned and tightened muscles, improvement in circulation and posture. Mentally, yoga can relieve chronic stress patterns, improve concentration and increase body awareness. Yoga can help improve conditions as serious as asthma, heart disease, arthritis and epilepsy.

Common misconceptions

'Yoga is too slow. It is too feminine for me.' Yoga may appear to be a feminine type of exercise but it provides exactly the types of exercise that will strengthen your core muscles (those around your trunk), take pressure off your back and tighten up the abdominal muscles. Ashtanga is the one to

go for if you want a powerful, physically demanding workout.

> **TIPS**
>
> - Seek out the class and style of yoga appropriate to your fitness level and needs.
> - Beware of instructors who have an abrupt or harsh teaching style.
> - Don't be afraid to discuss your particular needs (e.g. back pain or joint problems) with your yoga instructor. He or she will be able to advise you on an alternative set of exercises.

Difficulties in relaxing

Learning to relax can be problematic at times. Some of the most common problems encountered include:

- *Falling asleep*. Fine, if this is what you are aiming for, but if sleep is not what you are hoping to achieve you can lay down holding something unbreakable in your hand – if you doze off you would drop it and wake up.
- *Strange physical feelings*. These will inevitably occur if you are engaging in something physical you are not used to. It will take some practice before you begin to feel comfortable with the exercises and start naturally ignoring these sensations. Ensure that

you are not hyperventilating during the exercises or practising when you are starved or full, as this can trigger unpleasant sensations when you are trying to relax.

- *Unwanted thoughts*. These can pop up at any time and are normal. The best thing to do to get rid of them is to accept them. Try simply to focus on your exercises rather than thinking of the thoughts.
- *Excessive muscle tension*. This can lead to cramps, so ensure that you are not tensing your muscles too energetically. Remember to use a warm environment for your exercises and engage in them gently.

Appendix 2:

Improving sleep

The ability to sleep well should come naturally to us. However, it has been estimated that about 25 per cent of people are troubled by frequent insomnia. Among people with drinking problems the percentage is much higher. If your experience of sleep is exasperating, if your sleep is not soothing, if you spend a large part of your time in bed distressed because you cannot sleep, then a good chunk of your personal life (a third for most people) may well be unpleasant.

If drinking is the cause of your sleep problems or is contributing to them, you will have to learn how to sleep without using alcohol. Many people find that alcohol appears to help them get to sleep. Indeed, anything that induces relaxation will be helpful in stimulating sleep. The problem is that alcohol's effects go beyond inducing relaxation. Alcohol is a drug that interferes with the normal sleep cycle in a number of ways. If during sleep you have alcohol in your bloodstream you may well end up not getting enough of the deepest (and most restful) kind of sleep. In addition alcohol appears to increase the chances that a person will be agitated during sleep and will wake up more frequently during the night.

Not everyone who drinks experiences all of these effects, but in general although alcohol may help you fall asleep it will tend to cause marked sleep disturbances. It is also worth noting that when a person has become accustomed to drinking and then decreases it or stops using it, insomnia frequently occurs as part of the withdrawal from alcohol. If you are not aware of what is happening, you may be tempted to utilize alcohol again to get to sleep. This will only make the problem worse.

Falling asleep is a completely natural process. It is not something that you have to learn or relearn how to do. The natural progression from tiredness is to fall asleep unless there are obstacles that interfere with this process. Coping with insomnia, thus, is more a question of *removing obstacles* than of learning how to make yourself fall asleep. Things you can do include:

- *Relax*. The relaxation skills described in this book will be of help. Once you're relaxed physically, you may fall asleep naturally. The target is to focus on relaxing your body and your mind, not to make yourself go to sleep. Beware, thus, of practising relaxation *only* at bedtime, as you may unintentionally learn to feel sleepy whenever you relax. You might not find this desirable. Start by doing relaxation exercises at one other time during the day as well, when you're not getting ready to go to sleep.

- *Select a regular bedtime and waking time.* This is necessary because your body works best when you operate on predictable phases of activity and rest. It may also be helpful to plan your daily activities so that you begin to slow down as bedtime approaches. Avoid spending the hour before bedtime in pursuits that require thorough planning as this will usually escalate in thoughts or worries.
- *Make your sleep environment comfortable.* Reduce noise, darken the room, and arrange for a comfortable room temperature.
- *Don't use your bed for anything except sleeping.* Some people are perfectly capable of reading or watching TV in bed and then quickly falling asleep. But if you suffer from insomnia it can be distressing to lie awake desperately trying to get to sleep. If you don't fall asleep after a reasonable amount of time (10–25 minutes), get up, leave the bedroom and do something else until you feel sleepy. Then go straight back to bed, practice relaxation and allow yourself to fall asleep. Repeat if necessary.
- *Don't drink anything containing caffeine* within a few hours of your bedtime.
- *Don't drink alcohol* within 2 hours of going to bed.
- *Don't drink anything* just before going to bed so you won't have to wake up to go to the bathroom.
- *Don't smoke or use other drugs* within 2 hours of your bedtime.
- *Don't exercise* within 3 hours of your bedtime.

- *Don't have snacks* if you wake up in the middle of the night. You may learn to feel hungry in the middle of the night, and hunger can wake you up.

Remember that waking up in the middle of the night and not being able to get back to sleep is perfectly normal to a certain extent. The body goes through several stages of deep and light sleep, and sometimes in light sleep you wake up briefly. This seems to increase as you get older. The fact that you've woken up does not mean you'll stay awake.

Some sleep problems will require more extensive treatment. If you've tried relaxation for a few weeks, along with the other strategies mentioned in this chapter, but with no improvement, you may need to seek additional help.

Appendix 3:

Tackling worry

Worrying is a natural response to stressful life circumstances. If your worry leads you to creating solutions to the worrisome situation your worry is healthy. Here is an example:

Mary has an interview for a job she really wants and she is worried about the outcome. She decided to prepare really well. She has researched the company, prepared answers to possible questions, organized a mock interview with a friend and planned in advance what she is going to wear on the day.

Your worries can be classed as unhealthy if:

- your worry becomes all consuming
- you make decisions based on fears rather than on reason or logic
- you are chronically anxious about the future
- you overestimate the probability of bad things happening (i.e. catastrophize)
- you find yourself constantly asking 'What if X happens?'

Here is another example of unhealthy worry:

> *John constantly worries about the outcome of the interview. He finds waiting for it nerve-wracking. He fears that the panel of interviewers will not find him good enough and will not offer him the job. This will be catastrophic as he is in debt and behind in his rent. These thoughts have upset him so much that he cannot sleep at night. As a result, he is tired and cannot concentrate on anything, and he has hardly prepared for the interview.*

You can see in this example how unhealthy worry is preventing John from planning effective solutions to the problem. Paradoxically, he is unlikely to get the job not because of his lack of ability but because of the lack of preparation due to his unhealthy worry.

Common misconceptions

'Worry helps me cope.' This really is not the case. Think of the example above. Unnecessary worry takes away necessary resources to cope efficiently with the situation.

'If I worry bad things won't happen.' This is superstition. Things will happen whether we worry or not. The best we can do to improve our chances of good things happening is to problem solve where possible. Where this is not possible, we just have to let things unfold: simply wait and see!

TIPS WHICH WILL MAKE YOUR WORRISOME THOUGHTS MORE MANAGEABLE

- *Turn your worry into problem solving*. When you catch yourself going down the worry line, think problem solving. Ask yourself a question: What can I do to solve this problem?
- *Write your worries down*. The simple act of writing down your worries will make them less overwhelming.
- *Mindstorm for solutions*. Write down the solutions. Make a list of possible things that you could do to improve your situation. If you cannot come up with anything ask a friend to help you.
- *Evaluate each solution*. How realistic is it? Can you do it? What would it involve? What are the pros and cons?
- *Opt for the most realistic solution*. Decide on the best possible (i.e. realistic) solution and work out the steps necessary to put it into action. If you find that there really is no solution to your worry as it is completely outside of your control, it is probably not worth worrying about. Still, it may be difficult to switch off your mind. Try the next two exercises.
- *Interrupting 'what if' routines*. Become aware of the way your mind works.
- Notice when you begin to worry. You will start thinking 'What if X happens?' Inevitably X is something bad or undesirable.
- Interrupt the 'what if' routine. Tell yourself, 'There is nothing I can do about this situation. It is outside of my control. I am not going to worry about it.'
- It may be hard at first to put this into practice. However, if you have tried to problem solve your worry and you realize that it is largely outside of your control or that you have done all within your abilities to resolve the problem, it is important to give this technique a try.
- *Postponing worry*. Allocate some time each day to worry. For example, 30 minutes in the evening each day could be scheduled

in your diary as your 'worry time'. During your 'worry time' let your thoughts and worries roam free. Be strict with yourself. When a worry pop ups in your head during the day write it down and say to yourself that you will think about it during your 'worry time'. Be very rigid about this. Allow yourself to worry only during your allocated 'worry time'. Soon, you will realize that many worries are not worth worrying about. This exercise will help you contain your worry and reduce its impact on your life.

Appendix 4:

Dealing with anger

Anger (like anxiety, depression and worry) is a common human emotion. It tends to occur when we are not getting what we want and when things seem out of control. It is usually the consequences of anger (such as aggression, passivity and impulsive behaviors) that increase the likelihood of drinking. Research shows that people who have lapsed after a period of abstinence took their first drink when they were angry and upset. This is why it is important to learn to cope with anger and upset in a constructive way.

Common misconceptions

'I cannot control my anger.' As with other types of emotion, addressing activating events and thoughts will help to control anger. Anger does not just occur randomly. You may think that it is events or situations that make you angry, but in fact it is the thoughts about these situations and events that results in anger. The chain linking events, thoughts, emotions and behaviors can be summarized as in Figure A4.1.

Activating event ⟹ Thoughts ⟹ Emotions ⟹ Behavior

Figure A4.1 Chain linking events

TIPS WHICH WILL MAKE YOUR ANGER MORE MANAGEABLE

- Identify your activating events. The first step in managing your anger is to become conscious of your activating events. What is it that triggers your anger? Is it the frustration of not achieving a goal, a verbal insult, an obscene gesture, seeing someone else being attacked?
- Write down your anger-inducing thoughts. Try to become aware of the thoughts associated with anger. As we discussed in Chapter 15 any thought that is linked to an emotional reaction is likely to occur quickly and automatically, which is why you have to practice spotting your own 'bridging thoughts' to anger. Look at the example in Figure A4.2.

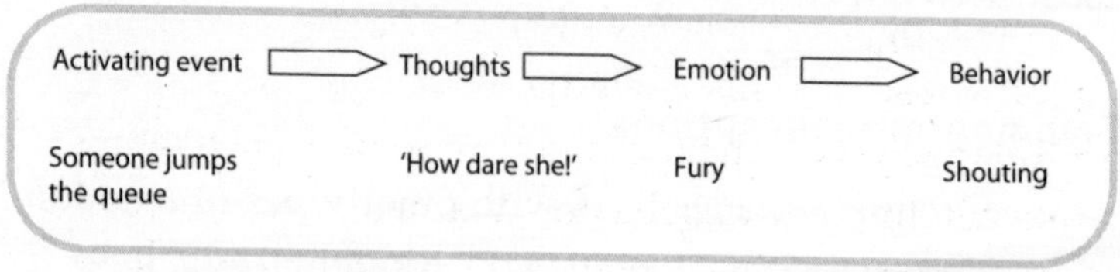

Activating event ⟹ Thoughts ⟹ Emotion ⟹ Behavior

| Someone jumps the queue | 'How dare she!' | Fury | Shouting |

Figure A4.2 Anger chain

Can you remember any thoughts that might be linked to episodes of anger in your life? You could begin with the following examples:

Activating event	Thoughts	Emotion
A driver cuts in front of you	....	Irritation
	....	
	....	
Somebody tells you are an idiot	....	Annoyance
	....	
	....	

- Change your thoughts about the activating event. Try to keep calm by saying to yourself 'relax' or 'take it easy'. Begin by questioning your interpretation of the situation. Are you overreacting? Is it that bad? Are there any other more constructive thoughts that could help you to feel less angry? Think about the negative consequences of getting angry (e.g. drinking). Replace the negative thoughts with more positive thoughts. Examples could include, 'Life is too short to get pissed off about anything'; 'He is not really trying to hurt me, he is just upset about something.'

- Change your behavior in response to the activating event. Implement behaviors that will make you feel calmer or will help you solve the problem. These can include:
  - being assertive enough to change your reaction to the situation
  - talking to the person associated with your anger in a slow and rational way
  - walking away from the situation.

There will be times when you will not be able to resolve the situation and you will still feel angry. Don't think about it over and over again as it will make you more upset. Engage in some pleasurable activity and try to distract yourself. If necessary call a friend and talk about it. Remember that all negative emotions will eventually subside if you do not attempt to control them (i.e. your anger will not last forever even though at the time it might feel like that).

Useful addresses

Problem drinking

UK and Eire Organizations
Addaction
67–69 Cowcross Street
London EC1M 6PU
Tel: 020 7251 5860
Fax: 020 7251 5890
Email: info@addaction.org.uk
Website: www.addaction.org.uk

Alcohol Concern
64 Leman Street
London E1 8EU
Tel: 020 7964 0510
Fax: 020 7488 9213
E-mail: contact@alcoholconcern.org.uk
Website: www.alcoholconcern.org.uk

Alcohol Drugs and Family (ADFAM)
25 Corsham Street
London N1 6DR
Tel: 020 7553 7640
Fax: 020 7253 7991
Email: admin@adfam.org.uk
Website: www.adfam.org.uk

Al-Anon Family Groups UK & Eire
61 Great Dover Street
London SE1 4YF
Tel: 020 7403 0888
Fax: 020 7378 9910
Email: enquiries@al-anonuk.org.uk
Website: www.al-anonuk.org.uk

Al-Anon information centres

Peace House
224 Lisburn Road
Belfast BT9 6GE
Northern Ireland
Tel: 028 9068 2368

Room 5
5 Capel Street
Dublin 1
EIRE
Tel: 00353 01 873 2699

Mansfield Park Building
Unit 6
22 Mansfield Street
Partick, Glasgow G11 5QP
Tel: 0141 339 8884 (24-hour helpline)

Hope UK (drugs education and prevention for young people)
25(F) Copperfield Street
London SE1 0EN
Tel: 020 7928 0848
Fax: 020 7401 3477
Email: enquiries@hopeuk.org
Website: www.hopeuk.org

Medical Council on Alcohol (MCA)
3 St Andrew's Place
Regent's Park
London NW1 4LB
Tel: 020 7487 4445
Fax: 020 7935 4479
Email: mca@medicouncilalcol.demon.co.uk
Website: www.medicouncilalcol.demon.co.uk

US Organizations
Alcoholics Anonymous
Website: www.aa.org

Moderation Management
Website: www.moderation.org

Secular Organizations for Sobriety
Website: www.secularsobriety.org

SMART Recovery
Website: www.smartrecovery.org

Women for Sobriety
Website: www.womenforsobriety.org

Cognitive Behavioral Therapy

UK Organizations
British Association for Behavioral and Cognitive Psychotherapies (BABCP)
Victoria Building
9-13 Silver Street
Bury BL9 0EU
Tel: 0161 797 4484
Fax: 0161 797 2670
Email: babcp@babcp.com
Website: www.babcp.com

British Psychological Society (BPS)
St Andrews House
48 Princess Road East
Leicester LE1 7DR
Tel: 0116 254 9568
Fax: 0116 227 1314
Email: enquiries@bps.org.uk
Website: www.bps.org.uk

Marcantonio Spada
Cognitive Behavior Therapy Centre
PO Box 649
28 Old Brompton Road
London SW7 3SS
Website: www.marcantoniospada.com

US Organizations
Albert Ellis Institute
Website: www.rebt.org

Association for Behavioral and Cognitive Therapies
Website: www.aabt.org

International Association for Cognitive Psychotherapy
Website: www.the-iacp.com

Counselling

British Association for Counselling and Psychotherapy (BACP)
BACP House
15 St John's Business Park
Lutterworth LE17 4HB
Tel: 01455 883300
Fax: 01455 550243
Email: bacp@bacp.co.uk
Website: www.bacp.co.uk

Relationship and family therapies

Association for Family Therapy and Systemic Practice (AFTSP)
7 Executive Suite
St James Court
Wilderspool Causeway
Warrington, Cheshire WA4 6PS
Tel: 01925 444 414
Email: s.kennedy@aft.org.uk
Website: www.aft.org.uk

Institute of Transactional Analysis (ITA)
Broadway House
149–151 St Neots Road
Hardwick, Cambridge CB23 7QJ
Wigton, CA7 9YH
Tel: 0845 0099 101
Fax: 0845 0099 202
Email: admin@ita.org.uk
Website: www.ita.org.uk

Relate: The Relationship People
Central Office
Premier House
Carolina Court
Lakeside, Doncaster DN4 5RA
Tel: 0300 100 1234
Email: enquiries@relate.org.uk
Website: www.relate.org.uk

References and further reading

For problem drinking

Ellis, A. (1975) *A Guide to Rational Living* (New York: Wilshire Book Company)

Goodwin, D. W. (2000) *Alcoholism: The Facts* (Oxford: Oxford University Press)

Miller, W. R. and Munoz, R. F. (2005) *Controlling your Drinking* (New York: Guilford Press)

Velleman, R. (1992) *Counselling for Alcohol Problems* (London: Sage Publications)

From the 'Overcoming' series for anxiety, stress, worry and depression

Butler, G. (1999) *Overcoming Social Anxiety and Shyness* (London: Constable & Robinson)

Davies, W. (2000) *Overcoming Anger and Irritability* (London: Constable & Robinson)

Fennell, M. (1999) *Overcoming Low Self-Esteem* (London: Constable & Robinson)

Gilbert, P. (2000) *Overcoming Depression* (London: Constable & Robinson)

Kennerley, H. (1997) *Overcoming Anxiety* (London: Constable & Robinson)

Scott, J. (2001) *Overcoming Mood Swings* (London: Constable & Robinson)

Extra exercise sheets, diaries, tables and figures

EXERCISE 1
PROBLEMS AND TARGETS

Problems	Targets

EXERCISE 2

ADVANTAGES OF CHANGING, CONCERNS, AND RESPONSES TO CONCERNS

Advantages	Concerns	Responses to concerns

Outcome

EXERCISE 3
EXAMINING SPECIFIC CHANGE CONCERNS

What do you predict will happen?

How likely is it to happen? (0–100%)

Evidence for	Evidence against

Outcome

How likely do you think it is now that this will happen? (0–100%)

Conclusions

EXERCISE 4
A-T-E-B-C ANALYSIS

Activating event	Thoughts	Emotions	Behaviors	Short-term consequences	Long-term consequences

EXERCISE 5
IDENTIFYING THE VICIOUS CYCLE

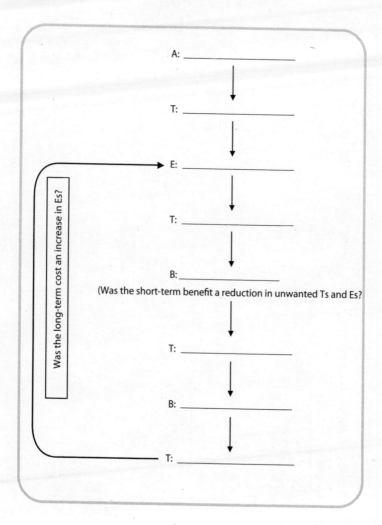

A: _____

T: _____

E: _____

T: _____

B: _____

(Was the short-term benefit a reduction in unwanted Ts and Es?

T: _____

B: _____

T: _____

Was the long-term cost an increase in Es?

EXERCISE 6
EVIDENCE FOR AND AGAINST UNCONTROLLABILITY THOUGHTS ABOUT DRINKING

Uncontrollability thoughts	Belief in each thought (0–100%)

Evidence for	Evidence against

Outcome

Rerating of belief in each thought (0–100%)

EXERCISE 7
HIERARCHY OF DIFFICULT SITUATIONS

Situation	Difficulty (0–100%)	Rank

EXERCISE 8
DRINKING POSTPONEMENT EXPERIMENT

Thought to be tested			Belief in the thought (0–100%)		
Experiment to test thought	Possible problems	Strategies to deal with problems	Date of experiment	Experiment outcome	Belief in the thought (0–100%)

EXERCISE 9

RECOGNIZING PERMISSIVE THOUGHTS ABOUT DRINKING

Activating event	Feelings and sensations	Permissive thoughts
When did it happen? Where were you? What were you doing? What were you thinking about?	What feelings and body sensations did you notice?	What were you saying to yourself that made it easier to keep drinking? Highlight the key thought that makes it most likely you will continue drinking.

EXERCISE 10
RECOGNIZING AND CHALLENGING PERMISSIVE THOUGHTS ABOUT DRINKING

Activating event	Feelings and sensations	Permissive thoughts	Evidence not supporting the thought	Alternative thought	Belief in alternative thought
When did it happen? Where were you? What were you doing? What were you thinking about?	What feelings and body sensations did you notice?	What were you saying to yourself that made it easier to keep drinking? Highlight the key thought that makes it most likely you will continue drinking.	Use the eight questions above to challenge your thought.	Note the alternative more helpful thought.	Rate how much you believe this thought to be true on a scale from 0–100%.

EXERCISE 11

IDENTIFYING POSITIVE THOUGHTS ABOUT DRINKING

Activating event	Feelings and sensations	Positive thoughts
When did it happen? Where were you? What were you doing? What were you thinking about?	What feelings and body sensations did you notice?	How did you think drinking would help? What were you afraid might happen if you did not drink?

EXERCISE 12
RECOGNIZING AND CHALLENGING POSITIVE THOUGHTS ABOUT DRINKING

Activating event	Feelings and sensation	Positive thoughts	Evidence not supporting the thought	Alternative thought	Belief in alternative thought
When did it happen? Where were you? What were you doing? What are you thinking about?	What feelings and body sensations did you notice?	What were you saying to yourself that made it easier to keep drinking? Highlight the key thought that makes it most likely to continue drinking.	Use the eight questions above to challenge your thought.	Note the alternative more helpful thought.	Rate how much you believe this thought to be true on a scale of 0–100%.

EXERCISE 13

EVIDENCE FOR AND AGAINST THE UNCONTROLLABILITY OF CRAVING

Craving thoughts	Belief in each thought (0–100%)		
Evidence for	Evidence against		
Outcome			
Rerating of belief in each thought (0–100%)			

EXERCISE 14

Understanding problem drinking

Building motivation to change

Implementing change

DRINKING DIARY

Date:	Morning	Units	Afternoon	Units	Evening	Units	Total units
Monday							
Tuesday							
Wednesday							
Thursday							
Friday							
Saturday							
Sunday							

Total units this week _____

ACTIVITY DIARY

Date: Sunday	Monday	Tuesday	Wednesday	Thursday	Friday	Saturday
9–10						
10–11						
11–12						
12–1						
1–2						
2–3						
3–4						
4–5						
5–6						
6–7						
7–12						

P = Pleasure (from 0 to 10)

DECISION SHEET

Preceding event/ situation	Apparently irrelevant decision	What could have been done differently	Pros of doing things differently	Cons of doing things differently	Safe alternative

HIGH-RISK SITUATIONS: WHAT TO DO

A DRINKING DECISION BALANCE SHEET			
Continuing to drink		Making a change in my drinking	
Benefits	Costs	Benefits	Costs

THE PROBLEM DRINKING MODEL

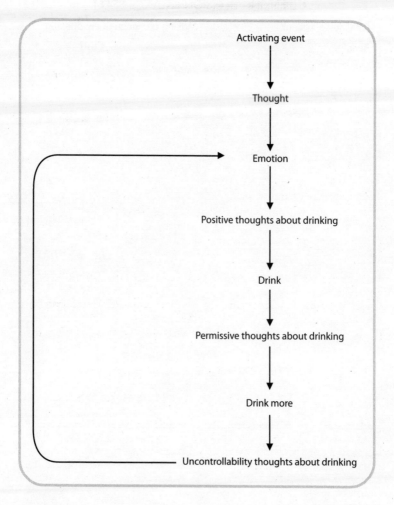

Index

More psychology titles from Constable & Robinson
Please visit www.overcoming.co.uk for more information

No.	Title	RRP	Offer price	Total
	An Introduction to Coping with Anxiety	£2.99	£2.00	
	An Introduction to Coping with Depression	£2.99	£2.00	
	An Introduction to Coping with Health Anxiety	£2.99	£2.00	
	An Introduction to Coping with Obsessive Compulsive Disorder	£2.99	£2.00	
	An Introduction to Coping with Panic	£2.99	£2.00	
	An Introduction to Coping with Phobias	£2.99	£2.00	
	Overcoming Anger and Irritability	£10.99	£8.99	
	Overcoming Anorexia Nervosa	£10.99	£8.99	
	Overcoming Anxiety	£10.99	£8.99	
	Overcoming Anxiety Self-Help Course (3 parts)	£21.00	£18.00	
	Overcoming Body Image Problems	£10.99	£8.99	
	Bulimia Nervosa and Binge-Eating	£10.99	£8.99	
	Overcoming Bulimia Nervosa and Binge-Eating Self-Help Course (3 parts)	£21.00	£18.00	
	Overcoming Childhood Trauma	£10.99	£8.99	
	Overcoming Chronic Fatigue	£10.99	£8.99	
	Overcoming Chronic Pain	£10.99	£8.99	
	Overcoming Compulsive Gambling	£10.99	£8.99	
	Overcoming Depersonalizaton and Feelings of Unreality	£10.99	£8.99	
	Overcoming Depression	£10.99	£8.99	
	Overcoming Depression: Talks With Your Therapist (audio)	£10.99	£8.99	
	Overcoming Grief	£10.99	£8.99	
	Overcoming Insomnia and Sleep Problems	£10.99	£8.99	
	Overcoming Low Self-Esteem	£10.99	£8.99	
	Overcoming Low Self-Esteem Self-Help Course (3 parts)	£21.00	£18.00	
	Overcoming Mood Swings	£10.99	£8.99	
	Overcoming Obsessive Compulsive Disorder	£10.99	£8.99	
	Overcoming Panic and Agoraphobia	£10.99	£8.99	
	Overcoming Panic and Agoraphobia Self-Help Course (3 parts)	£21.00	£18.00	
	Overcoming Paranoid and Suspicious Thoughts	£10.99	£8.99	

More psychology titles from Constable & Robinson (*continued*)

No.	Title	RRP	Offer price	Total
	Overcoming Problem Drinking	£10.99	£8.99	
	Overcoming Relationship Problems	£10.99	£8.99	
	Overcoming Sexual Problems	£10.99	£8.99	
	Overcoming Social Anxiety and Shyness	£10.99	£8.99	
	Overcoming Social Anxiety and Shyness Self-Help Course (3 parts)	£21.00	£18.00	
	Overcoming Traumatic Stress	£10.99	£8.99	
	Overcoming Weight Problems	£10.99	£8.99	
	Overcoming Worry	£10.99	£8.99	
	Overcoming Your Child's Fears and Worries	£10.99	£8.99	
	Overcoming Your Child's Shyness and Social Anxiety	£10.99	£8.99	
	Overcoming Your Smoking Habit	£10.99	£8.99	
	The Happiness Trap	£9.99	£7.99	
	The Glass Half-Full	£8.99	£7.99	
	I Had a Black Dog	£6.99	£5.24	
	Living with a Black Dog	£7.99	£5.99	
	Manage Your Mood: How to use Behavioral Activation Techniques to Overcome Depression	£12.99	£9.99	
	P&P		FREE	FREE
	TOTAL			

Name (block letters): _____

Address: _____

_____   Postcode: _____

Email: _____   Tel No: _____

How to Pay:

1. **By telephone**: call the TBS order line on **01206 255 800** and quote **CRBK10**. Phone lines are open between Monday–Friday, 8.30am–5.30pm.

2. **By post**: send a cheque for the full amount payable to TBS Ltd, and send form to:
Freepost RLUL-SJGC-SGKJ. Cash Sales/Direct Mail Dept, The Book Service, Colchester Road, Frating, Colchester, CO7 7DW

Is/are the book(s) intended for personal use ☐ or professional use ☐?
Please note this information will not be passed on to third parties.

Constable & Robinson Ltd (directly or via its agents) may mail or phone you about promotions or products Tick box if you do not want these from us ☐ or our subsidiaries ☐